JUST
LIKE
JESUS

God loves you just the way you are,

but he refuses to leave you that way.

He wants you to be . . .

JUST LIKE JESUS

max lucado

with teen story adaptations by MONICA HALL

Tommy nelson™
A Division of Thomas Nelson, Inc.

www.tommynelson.com
www.ThomasNelson.com

Published in Nashville, Tennessee, by Tommy Nelson®, a Division of Thomas Nelson, Inc.

Karen Hill, Administrative Editor for Max Lucado.

Interior design by Brecca Theele.

Scripture quotations noted NCV used in this book are from the Holy Bible, New Century Version®, copyright © 1987, 1988,
1991 by W Publishing Group, Nashville, Tennessee 37214. Used by permission.

Other Scripture references are used by permission from the following sources: The International Children's Bible®, New
Century Version® (ICB), copyright © 1986, 1989, 1999 by Tommy Nelson®, a Division of Thomas Nelson, Inc. The Good
News Bible: Today's English Version (TEV), copyright © 1966, 1971, 1976 by the American Bible Society. The Holy Bible,
New International Version (NIV), copyright © 1973, 1978, 1984 by New York International Bible Society, Zondervan Bible
Publishers. J. B. Phillips: The New Testament in Modern English, Revised Edition (PHILLIPS), copyright © J. B. Phillips 1958,
1960, 1972 by The Macmillan Company. The Jerusalem Bible (TJB), copyright © 1968 by Darton, Longman, & Todd, Ltd.,
and Doubleday & Co., Inc. The King James Version of the Bible (KJV). The Living Bible (TLB), copyright © 1971 by Tyndale
House Publishers. The Message (MSG), copyright © 1993, 1994, 1995 by Eugene H. Peterson, NavPress Publishing
Group. New American Standard Bible (NASB), copyright © 1960, 1977 by the Lockman Foundation. The New King James
Version (NKJV), copyright © 1979, 1980, 1982 by Thomas Nelson, Inc. The New Revised Standard Version Bible (NRSV),
copyright © 1989 by the Division of Christian Education of the National Council of the Churches of Christ in the U.S.A.
The Revised Standard Version of the Bible (RSV), copyright © 1946, 1952, 1971, 1973 by the Division of Christian
Education of the National Council of the Churches of Christ in the USA.

The information about Frank Laubach in chapter 6 is from Brother Lawrence and Frank Laubach, *Practicing His Presence*
(Goleta, Calif.: Christian Books, 1973). Used by the kind permission of Dr. Robert S. Laubach and Gene Edwards.

The information about William Rathje in chapter 11 is from Jim Morrison, "Slightly Rotted Gold," *American Way Magazine*,
1 April 1992, 32–35.

Library of Congress Cataloging-in-Publication Data

Lucado, Max
     Just like Jesus / Max Lucado ; with teen story adaptations by Monica Hall.
       p. cm.
     Based on Just Like Jesus by Max Lucado.
     Summary: A collection of stories of everyday life, with commentary, designed to help one develop a forgiving heart,
  a willing heart, an enduring heart, and otherwise become more like Jesus.
     ISBN: 1-4003-0160-2
     1. Christian teenagers—Religious life—Juvenile literature. 2. Christian life—Juvenile literature. [1. Teenagers—
  Religious life. 2. Christian life. 3. Conduct of life.] I. Hall, Monica. II. Title.

  BV4531.3 .L83 2002
  248.8'3—dc21   2002043203

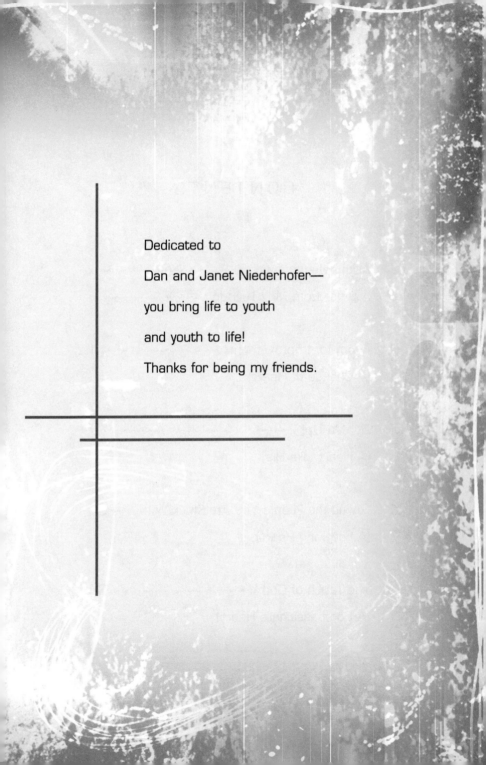

Dedicated to

Dan and Janet Niederhofer—

you bring life to youth

and youth to life!

Thanks for being my friends.

CONTENTS

ACKNOWLEDGMENTS

Way to go Laura Minchew, Beverly Phillips, and June Ford!
Loud applause for you, Monica Hall!
Karen Hill—you're awesome!
Bryan Hines, Lanie Holbrook, and Sammie Mechinus—thanks
    for your "tween" perspective!
And God, you're the One and Only!

Dear Friend,

To spend these moments with you is a high privilege, and I want you to know how grateful I am for the opportunity. Within this book, you and I are going to seek out the compassion of God and through it discover his great love. After all, you are God's project . . . his magnum opus . . . his "great work."

And although God loves you just the way you are, he refuses to leave you that way. He wants you to be just like Jesus. He wants you to have a heart like his. That is God's desire and the theme of this book.

My prayer for you is this: May God open your eyes so that you can see Jesus. And in seeing Jesus, may you see what you are called to be.

Max Lucado

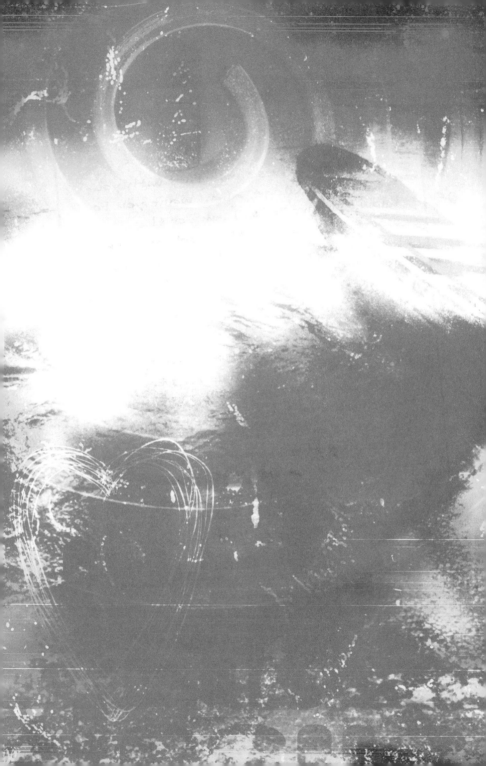

1 | ROOM FOR IMPROVEMENT

(A CHANGE OF HEART)

Create in me a pure heart,
O God, and renew a
steadfast spirit within me.
　　　—PSALM 51:10 NIV

› › › Caitlin was going to miss her big sister when Molly left for college. Really. She *would.* (But, goodness, it certainly was taking Molly long enough to actually leave!)

Time to move things along, Caitlin thought—ruthlessly jamming a stack of clothes into the last open suitcase. "Here, Moll, let me give you a hand. Mom and Dad are ready."

Molly looked at her sister with a twinkle in her green eyes. "Not trying to get rid of me, are you?" she asked, then smiled.

"Me?" Eyes as green as Molly's own looked back— eyes positively *overflowing* with mischievousness. Then Caitlin grinned. "Well, you know . . ."

Molly did know. It was a Kelly family tradition. The oldest daughter at home got The Room—the absolutely *fantastic* remodeled attic—as her very own. First it was Diedre's room. Then Molly's. Now it was Caitlin's turn. (And six-year-old Megan was probably already making *her* plans!)

"I'm going . . . I'm going," Molly said with a laugh, dragging her bags over to the spiral staircase—where she nearly tripped over a stack of Caitlin's art supplies, which had "moved in" *slightly* early.

"Oops. Sorry," said Caitlin, following with Molly's overstuffed duffel—and one last glance around the room she'd been waiting to get for practically *forever*. Hers, all hers. And it was perfect! Or would be—with just a few minor "improvements."

My writing room is different than it used to be. Just a few months ago these walls were white. Now they are green. Once these windows were curtain covered; today they wear shutters. My chair used to sit on a tan carpet, which is now white. Actually, I had no problem with the tan carpet. Nor did I object to white walls and curtains. From my perspective the room looked fine.

But not from my wife's perspective. Denalyn loves to decorate. Better stated, she *has* to decorate. She can no more leave a house unchanged than an artist can leave a canvas untouched or a musician a song unsung. For Denalyn it's not enough to own a house; she has to change the house.

As for me, I'm content with owning the house. My tastes are, shall we say, less . . . particular. Give me a chair and a refrigerator and I'm happy. For me the big job is buying the house. Once that's done, I'm ready to move in and rest.

Not Denalyn. As the ink is drying on the deed, she is moving in and remodeling. I wonder if she inherited this trait from her Father . . . her heavenly Father. You see, the way Denalyn views a house is the way God views a life.

God loves to decorate. God *has* to decorate. Let him live long enough in a heart, and that heart will begin to change. Portraits of hurt will be replaced by landscapes of grace. Walls of anger will be demolished and shaky foundations restored. God can no more leave a life unchanged than a mother can leave her child's tear untouched.

> The way Denalyn views a house is the way God views a life.

It's not enough for him to own you; he wants to change you. Where you and I might be satisfied with a recliner and a refrigerator, he refuses to settle for any dwelling short of a palace. After all, your heart is his house. No expense is spared. No corners are cut. "Oh, the utter extravagance of his work in us who trust him" (Ephesians 1:18–19 MSG).

› › › With a final sweep of indigo paint, Caitlin finished the rainbow. She *loves* rainbows, always has—ever since she first heard her mother call them "God's promises." Her eyes traced the soft bands of color that arced up from her bed into the "sky" she'd created overhead. *Wait till Molly sees this!*

And it was worth seeing. She'd spent every spare moment—and many she *shouldn't* have spared—that autumn transforming The Room. Painting the slanted ceiling the palest blue, then sponging on fluffy white clouds. Creating a nest of colorful pillows for the cozy window seat that looked out into the treetops. Filling the wall of shelves with her books and treasures. And next week she'd finally begin painting the fantasy forest on the wall opposite her bed. It would be like waking up every day in one of her favorite books!

Yes, her redecorating was coming right along. Then Caitlin frowned. Something—*something*—seemed to be missing. And she had no idea what.

> *Caitlin frowned. Something— something— seemed to be missing.*

› › › › › › › › › › › ›

Caitlin finished painting the last tree on her "forest" wall early in November. There! The Room was fin-

ROOM FOR IMPROVEMENT

ished. Sort of. She *still* hadn't figured out what it was that was *missing*. Until her birthday present from Molly arrived.

Happy Birthday, Little Sis.
Can hardly wait for Thanksgiving to see all the changes you've made in The Room. (You're probably up to your eyebrows in paint!)
But first . . . your b-day present. Knew this was for you the moment I saw it at the arts festival. Just a reminder that beautiful <u>outsides</u> begin with beautiful <u>insides</u>—and that every space needs a "heart."
                    Love,
                    Molly

Inside the brightly wrapped package was the most beautiful keepsake box Caitlin had ever seen. Hand-painted on the lid was a misty forest of tall, graceful trees, with sunlight slanting streaks of gold through rain-drenched branches. It was almost as if the artist had had a ringside seat on the third day of Creation.

But it was what was *inside* the incredible box that really took her breath away. Inside, the same talented hand had swashed a joyous rainbow across the soft leather cover of a Bible.

"Oh, my," breathed Caitlin, "God's promises." That was it! That's what had been missing. No wonder she'd felt so . . . uncomfortable. She'd been so busy pleasing herself with outside changes that she'd seriously neglected the truly important *inside* things. But that could change. In fact, wasn't she an *expert* at change? Especially now that—thanks to Molly—her heart was in the right place.

Humming softly to herself, Caitlin placed her sister's gift—and the promises it held—on her bedside table. Then she looked around The Room, and smiled. *Perfect!*

God's determination to change and beautify what he owns might explain some of the discomfort in your life when you are faced with tough choices about attitude, honesty, or morality. Remodeling of the heart is not always pleasant . . . or painless. Sometimes you forget who is at work in your life, and what he wants for you.

Your Creator has high goals for you. He is remaking you into the image of Christ. *He wants you to be just like Jesus!* This is God's desire and passion and plan for you. You are God's *project* . . . his magnum opus . . . his "great work."

Remodeling of the heart is not always pleasant.

2 | LIGHTEN UP!

(A HEART LIKE HIS)

Arise, shine,
for your light has come,
and the glory of the LORD
rises upon you.
　　　　—ISAIAH 60:1 NIV

›　›　› If ever there was a person who *had* to know what made things "tick," it was Andrew C. (for Curiosity) Clark. His first word was "why," followed quickly by "how." But it was when he added "what if" to his vocabulary that things *really* got interesting.

What if . . . pieces of this *toy and parts from* that *gadget were put together? What if . . . I could make my remote-control car fly? What if . . . I could rig my tooth-brush so it would remind me to brush? What if . . .*

Well, you get the idea.

With a dash of imagination and a little tinkering, Andrew could "improve" just about *anything*—with some pretty lively results. His family never knew what to expect when Andrew handed them a gift. Would it be the spring-loaded checkers that "jumped" by themselves or the hamster-powered alarm clock that set off bells, whistles, and waving flags with the small pet's first nibble of the day? And his sister was *still* recovering from the jet-powered hairbrush he gave her for Christmas!

Andrew's inventions made living in the Clark house something of an adventure—and led, through the years, to some truly amazing science fair projects at school. Andrew loved being the star of the class at those times. But once the event was over, everyone seemed to forget his cool projects and, even worse, forget *him* altogether. The truth was, he didn't have *any* friends.

Yes, when it came to making crazy contraptions, Andrew knew exactly what he was doing. But when it came to making friends, he just didn't have a clue how to go about it. It seemed so easy for guys like Mark Evans, the class president. Which started Andrew wondering—after all, if he could figure out what made complicated contraptions work, he should

. . . when it came to making friends, he just didn't have a clue . . .

be able to figure out how to make friends! *Maybe if I think about it the same way I troubleshoot inventions, I could figure this out, too.* **Why** *does everyone like Mark so much?* **How** *does he do it?* **What if** *I could discover his secret and make it work for me?*

And with that, another Andrew C. Clark project was under way.

°**"What if . . . ?"** Two simple little words that have been the starting point for discovery, solutions, and transformation, ever since humans first had two brain cells to rub together. "What if" thinking has given us in-line skates, men on the moon, and Web sites that connect us to anywhere in the world in seconds. Now just imagine for a minute what that kind of thinking can do when it comes to people! Imagine what your life could be like if you chose the most perfect of all role models and then added "what if." Think about it:

What if, for one day, Jesus were to live your life?

What if, for twenty-four hours, Jesus wakes up in your bed, walks in your shoes, lives in your house, does what you do? Your homework becomes his homework, your parents become his parents, your problems become his problems. Nothing in your life changes, except for *one* thing—your heart. For one day and one night, Jesus lives *your* life with *his* heart.

What would Jesus-as-you be like? Would your family, your

friends notice a change? Would you treat people the same way? Would the same things be important to you? Would you still *do* what you are doing? Would the heart of Christ be more forgiving than your own heart?

First, think about your plans for the next twenty-four hours. "See" yourself *being* yourself—at school, at home, with friends. Visualize the way you'll probably deal with the choices, the challenges, the opportunities you'll face. Then ask yourself this: *With Jesus taking over my heart, would anything change?*

Take your time. Adjust the lens of your imagination until you have a clear picture of Jesus leading *your* life. Then snap the picture and frame it. What you see is what God wants. He wants you to "think and act like Christ Jesus" (Philippians 2:5 NCV).

> › › › Andrew's new project turned out to be a lot more complicated than he had expected.
>
> *Doesn't this guy Mark ever stay* still*?!*
>
> Andrew was used to working with *things*—which tended to stay neatly in one place.
>
> Mark, on the other hand, was here, there, everywhere! In motion, but not really in a rush. Busy, but never *too* busy for the things (a lot of them) and the people (most all of them) he thought were important.
>
> When Mark showed up, people noticed—and they were always glad to see him. But he never seemed to do anything special to make that happen.

> *Figuring this out is not going to be easy,* thought Andrew. But he loved a challenge. And, fortunately, he had a plan.

God's plan for you is nothing short of a new heart. If you were a car, God would tune up your engine. If you were a computer, he would upgrade your hard drive. But since you're a person, God wants to change your heart.

God wants you to be just like Jesus. He wants you to have a heart like his.

If we could capture God's desire for each of us in a sentence or two, it would probably read like this:

> *God loves you just the way you are,*
> *but he refuses to leave you that way.*
> *He wants you to be just like Jesus.*

God loves you just the way you are. If you think his love for you would be stronger if your faith were stronger, you are wrong. If you think his love would be deeper if your thoughts were deeper, wrong again. Don't confuse God's love with the love of people. Human love often increases with performance and decreases with mistakes. Not so with God's love. He loves you right where you are.

God loves you just the way you are, but . . . he refuses to leave you that way! It's what a father *does*.

It's what *I* did, that day in the park when my daughter

Jenna was just a toddler playing in the sandbox. I'd only turned my back for a minute to buy her a treat from the ice-cream man. But when I turned around again, there sat my "angel," beaming at me—with her mouth full of sand!

Did I love her with dirt in her mouth? Absolutely. Was she any less my daughter with dirt in her mouth? Of course not. Was I going to allow her to keep the dirt in her mouth? No way. I loved her right where she was, but I refused to leave her there. I carried her over to the water fountain and washed out her mouth. Why? Because I love her.

God does the same for us. He holds us over the fountain. "Spit out the dirt, honey," our Father urges, "I've got something better for you." And so he cleanses us of filth, dishonesty, unkindness, bitterness, greed. We don't enjoy the cleansing; sometimes we even choose the dirt over the ice cream.

"I can eat dirt if I want to!" we pout. Which is true—we can. But if we do, the loss is ours. God has a better offer. He wants us to be just like Jesus.

Isn't that good news? You aren't stuck with today's personality. You aren't condemned to "grumpydom." You are tweakable. Even if you've worried every day of your life, you don't have to worry the rest of your life. So what if you were born a "Gloomy Gus"? You don't have to die one.

Where did we get the idea we can't change? When did we learn to say, "It's just my nature to worry" or "I can't help my bad temper"? Who says?!

> **Where did we get the idea we can't change?**

Would we say the same things about our bodies? "It's just my nature to have a broken leg. I can't do anything about it." Of course not. If our bodies malfunction, we seek help. Shouldn't we do the same with our hearts? Can't we seek aid for our sour attitudes, our selfish tirades? Of course we can. Jesus can change our hearts. He wants us to have a heart like his.

Can you imagine a better offer?

> > > *Maybe I need a better plan,* thought Andrew, from his observation post in the bleachers at track practice. His original plan—managing to accidentally-on-purpose be every place Mark Evans was for one week—wasn't working out all that well.

First of all, keeping up with Mark wasn't exactly easy. The pace of Mark's routine at school was tough, but his activities after school and through the weekend were nothing less than *exhausting!*

Even worse, here it was already Tuesday—Day 6!—and he was no closer to the "secret" than when he started! All he had was a few notes that told him . . . absolutely nothing.

Sure, that famous Mark smile and friendly "Hi" got a *lot* of use . . . and not just for his buddies. You didn't have to be "popular" or "important" to be noticed by Mark. In fact, he seemed to go out of his way for people who weren't so popular—like that new kid he'd invited to lunch on Friday.

But, hey, anybody could do that. (Although Andrew never had.)

Oh, and add a great sense of humor to the list. Mark was lightning fast with a clever remark, but he never laughed *at* anyone. And though kids hung on his every word, he actually—and this *was* interesting—listened more than he talked. Really *listened.*

But anybody could do that, too! (Unless, like Andrew, they happened to be thinking about something *else* at the time.)

〉 〉 〉 〉 〉 〉 〉 〉 〉 〉 〉 〉

The more Andrew studied his notes, the more Mark looked like just an ordinary kid. On the other hand . . . he *did* seem to spend a lot of time doing things he didn't really *have* to—mowing the lawn free for an elderly neighbor, walking dogs at the animal shelter, helping with the youth group car wash. And that was just last Saturday!

But it was what was happening today at track practice that *really* impressed Andrew.

Wow, look at them go! . . . Andrew held his breath as Joe Carter and Mark raced down the track side by side, neither giving an inch. The two friends—and fierce rivals—had trained all season for this time trial. At stake was a starting slot at Friday's regional meet.

Gonna be close . . . Oh, no! The two moving bodies were trying to occupy the *same* space. After a desperate struggle for balance, Mark caught his stride and raced on, but Joe fell down—and stayed down.

Now there was nothing between Mark and the finish line. The race was his. Until he *turned back*, and dashed to his motionless friend! "You okay, Joe?"

Andrew was stunned. So was Sam Reilly, the way-back-in-third-place runner who would now be starting for his school at regionals!

Wow, thought an awed Andrew, *I'm not sure I'd have the* heart *to do that!*

> That's what it's all about: heart.
> Jesus' heart. Your heart.

The Heart of Jesus

The heart of Jesus was **pure**. He was adored by thousands, yet content to live a simple life. He was scorned by his own creation, but willing to forgive them before they even asked. After spending three and a half years with Jesus, Peter described him as a "lamb unblemished and spotless" (1 Peter 1:19 NASB) and John concluded, "And in him is no sin" (1 John 3:5 NIV).

Jesus' heart was **peaceful**. The disciples fretted over how to feed the thousands, but not Jesus. He thanked God for the problem. The disciples shouted out of fear in the storm, but not Jesus. He slept through it. Peter drew his sword to fight the soldiers, but not Jesus. He lifted his hand to heal.

When his disciples abandoned him, did he pout and go home? When Peter denied him, did Jesus lose his temper? When the soldiers spit in his face, did he breathe fire in theirs? Far from it. He forgave them. His heart was at peace.

> *He forgave them. His heart was at peace.*

Jesus refused to be guided by anything other than his high call. His heart was **purposeful.** Most lives aim at nothing in particular . . . and achieve it. Jesus aimed at one goal—to save humanity from its sin. Jesus was so focused on his task that he knew when to say, "My time has not yet come" (John 2:4 NCV) and when to say, "It is finished" (John 19:30 NCV). But he was *not* so focused on his goal that he was unpleasant.

Quite the contrary. How **pleasant** were his thoughts! He could find beauty in lilies, joy in worship, and possibilities in problems. He spent more than thirty years wading through the muck of our sin, yet still saw enough beauty in us to die for our mistakes.

But the crowning quality of Jesus was this: His heart was **spiritual.** His thoughts reflected his intimate relationship with the Father. "I am in the Father and the Father is in me," he stated (John 14:11 NCV). He was "led by the Spirit" (Matthew 4:1 NIV). Jesus took his instructions from God. The heart of Jesus was spiritual.

The Heart of Humanity

Our hearts seem so far from his. He is pure; we are greedy. He is peaceful; we are hassled. He has a purpose; we are distracted. He is pleasant; we are cranky. He is spiritual; we are earthbound. The distance between our hearts and his seems so enormous. How could we ever hope to have the heart of Jesus?

Ready for a surprise? **You already do.** You already have the heart of Christ. If you are in Christ, you already have the heart of Christ! He has made your heart his home. Paul explains it with these words: "Strange as it seems, we Christians actually do have within us a portion of the very thoughts and mind of Christ" (1 Corinthians 2:16 TLB).

Strange is the word! If we have the mind and heart of Jesus, why do we still have the same old thoughts and hang-ups?

Could it be because we're connected to the power, but aren't *using* it? Kind of like being wired for electricity, and living by candlelight. Connected . . . but not *altered*.

Don't we make that same mistake when it comes to God? We, too—with our souls saved but our hearts unchanged—are connected but not altered. Trusting Christ to save us, but resisting the change that goes along with it. Oh, once in a while we'll flip the switch and enjoy the light, but most of the time we settle for puttering about in the shadows.

What would happen if we left the power on? What would

happen if we not only flipped the switch but *lived* in the light? What changes would occur if we let the radiance of Christ power our lives?

> ❯ ❯ ❯ Andrew was as much in the dark as ever on Day 7 . . . and—*Oh, no!*—now he'd lost sight of his subject, too!

He rushed down the school hall, zipped around the corner, and bumped right into . . . Mark Evans!

"Okay, Andrew Clark . . . what's up? Why have I developed a shadow this past week?"

"You, uh, you know who I am?!" Andrew was flabbergasted.

"Well, of course," said Mark with an admiring grin, "the guy with the really cool science projects." One eyebrow rose. "Wait a minute . . . please tell me I'm not one of them."

"Well . . . ," Andrew began. His explanation came out a little jumbled, but he got the idea across.

Mark gave him a long look. Then he smiled. "Sorry to put a kink in your 'project,' but there *is* no secret. I just ask myself how *I'd* like to be treated, then that's what I do." He looked at his watch. "Oops, gotta run. Promised Sam Reilly I'd help him get ready for regionals. Sorry I couldn't be more help."

. . . the big "secret" was the well-known (but not-so-well-used) Golden Rule!

Andrew did a great imitation of a rock for a while—not moving a muscle. Just thinking. Then he grinned. Imagine that . . . the big "secret" was the well-known (but not-so-well-*used*) Golden Rule!

Just treat others the way I'd like to be treated. Well, I could do that! And he did. Which turned out to be the very *best* plan of all.

God has big plans for you. The same one who saved your soul longs to remake your heart. His plan is nothing short of a total transformation: "He decided from the outset to shape the lives of those who love him along the same lines as the life of his Son" (Romans 8:29 MSG).

God is willing to change you into the likeness of the Savior. Will you accept his offer? Will you "fix your eyes on Jesus" . . . and explore the glorious "What if . . ." of letting God's light shine in *you?*

3

LOVING THE PEOPLE YOU ARE STUCK WITH

(A FORGIVING HEART)

Be gentle and ready to forgive;
never hold grudges. Remember,
the Lord forgave you, so you
must forgive others.
      —COLOSSIANS 3:13 TLB

› › › Almost no one had expected it to work. Kate and Courtney? *Sisters?!* (Okay, *step*sisters.) Two years later, no one—including Kate and Courtney—could explain how or why it *did* work.

A nationwide search would not find two thirteen-year-olds who were *less* alike. Practical, down-to-earth, athletic—and superorganized—Kate. Flighty, fashionable, artistic—and totally absent-minded—Courtney.

It was hard to picture them in the same universe, let alone the same blended family. But there they were, stuck with each other—and, amazingly, actually seeming to enjoy it. Usually. Although there *were* times—like Tuesday morning—when things got a little . . . hairy.

My first pet was a childhood Christmas Eve gift. Somewhere I have a snapshot of a brown-and-white Chinese pug, small enough to fit in my father's hand, cute enough to steal my eight-year-old heart. We named her Liz.

I carried her all day. Her floppy ears fascinated me, and her flat nose amused me. I even took her to bed. So what if she smelled like a dog? I thought the odor was cute. So what if she whined and whimpered? I thought the noise was cute. So what if she did her business on my pillow? I can't say I thought that was cute, but I didn't mind.

In our pre-dog discussions, Mom and Dad had made it clear that I was to be Liz's caretaker, and I was happy to agree. When she came home, I cleaned her little eating dish and opened her can of puppy food. The minute she lapped up some water, I refilled it. I kept her hair combed and her tail wagging.

Within a few days, however, my feelings changed a bit. Liz was still my dog, and I was still her friend, but I grew tired of her barking, and she seemed hungry an awful lot. More than once my folks had to remind me, "Take care of her. She is your dog."

I didn't like hearing those words—*your dog.* I wouldn't have minded "your dog to play with" or "your dog when you want her" or even "your dog when she is behaving." But those weren't my parents' words. They said, "Liz is *your dog*." Period. In sickness and in health. For richer, for poorer. In dryness and in wetness.

That's when it occurred to me: *I am stuck with Liz.* The courtship was over, and the honeymoon had ended. We were mutually leashed. Liz went from an option to an obligation, from a pet to a chore, from someone to play with to someone to care for.

Sound familiar? That "trapped" feeling that comes with being in a situation you can't escape? Only instead of being reminded, "She is your dog," you're told, "He is your brother." Or, "She is your lab partner, math teacher, picky-aunt-who-means-well . . ." or any other relationship that requires loyalty for survival.

Such permanence can lead to panic—at least it did in me. I had to answer some tough questions. Can I put up with the same flat-nosed, hairy, hungry face every morning? Am I going to be barked at until the day I die? Will she always use the inside of the house as a bathroom?

Stuckititis

Such are the questions we ask when we feel stuck with someone. There is a word for this condition. Upon consulting the one-word medical dictionary (which I wrote the day before I did this chapter), I discovered this is a common ailment known as *stuckititis* **(STUK-ih-TITE-is).** Read it out loud: *stuckititis.* Here's what *Max's Manual of Medical Terms* has to say about the condition:

Attacks of *stuckititis* are limited to people who breathe, and typically occur somewhere between birth and death. *Stuckititis* shows itself in irritability, short fuses, and a mountain range of molehills.

The always-helpful *Max's Manual* identifies three ways to cope with stuckititis: **flee, fight,** or **forgive.**

Some choose to flee: give up on the friendship, teammate, teacher, or family member by avoiding that person or quitting the team or changing schools. Though they are often surprised when the condition seems to follow them there, too. Others fight: snapping, complaining, arguing, and just generally making life miserable for everyone. A few, however, discover another treatment: forgiveness. (Forgiveness: Part patience and understanding. Part generosity. *All* love.)

My manual has no model for how forgiveness occurs . . . but the Bible does.

> › › › When Kate's mom and Courtney's dad began dating a little more than two years ago, neither girl paid much attention. By the time they realized wedding bells were in the air, it was too late to protest. Not that either wanted to. Kate really liked Courtney's dad, who was funny and kind—and a real soccer nut. And Courtney *adored* Kate's mom, who was sweet and understanding—and a world-class shopper!

About each other, the jury was still out. They had absolutely nothing in common, completely different circles of friends, and no idea what made the other tick. On the other hand, it might be kind of . . . interesting.

Fortunately, it was a big house, with plenty of personal space for when the girls needed a breather from working out their "sisterly" relationship. As it turned out, it wasn't all that difficult—once they realized you didn't necessarily have to get all bent out of shape about differences.

Some differences, in fact, were funnier than they were annoying. Others surprisingly "educational." The rest you just put up with, bearing in mind that your own quirks might be a little aggravating, too.

Though Kate did have to work at not cracking up every time she stepped into Ruffle City (Courtney's ultrafeminine, stuff-everywhere room). And Courtney had to swallow any number of comments about Kate's approach to fashion (Ignore it and maybe it'll go away!).

They had absolutely nothing in common . . .

On the other hand, if it hadn't been for Courtney's passion for dance, Kate would never have known that ballet demanded so much work and focus and . . . sweat. (Why, it was practically . . . *athletic!*) And Courtney was astonished at the clever footwork, driving pace, and intricate patterns of play when she saw her first soccer game. ("Why, it's like a . . . *dance!*")

Not that there wasn't some occasional teeth grinding. Getting Courtney anywhere on time—or through the mall without a gazillion detours—was as frustrating as trying to herd cats. And Kate's "fixation" on schedules and deadlines sometimes got on Courtney's *very last* nerve.

There is, however, more than *one* way around any block. So Kate learned to allow extra time when she and Courtney went places together. And Courtney tried hard to remember to actually *read* Kate's frequent reminder notes.

And so it went. Cut a little slack here. Make an allowance there. Hang on to your sense of humor. And learn to say—with a smile—"Well, that's Kate/Courtney."

And it pretty much worked. Right up until Tuesday morning. When a casual comment at breakfast revealed that Kate's soccer awards banquet and Courtney's dance recital (which everyone *thought* was next week) were *both* scheduled for Friday. At the same time. And each girl wanted/expected/needed a supportive, full-family audience!

Which meant that—unless someone could figure out how to be two places at once—they were definitely . . . stuck.

Jesus himself knew the feeling of being stuck with someone. For three years he ran with the same crew. By and large, he saw the same dozen or so faces around the table, around the campfire, around the clock. They rode in the same boats and walked the same roads and visited the same houses, and I wonder, how did Jesus stay so devoted to his men?

Not only did he have to put up with their visible oddities, he had to endure their invisible quirks. Think about it. He could hear their unspoken thoughts. He knew their private doubts. Not only that, he knew their *future* doubts. What if you knew every mistake your loved ones had ever made and every mistake they would ever make? What if you knew every thought they would have about you, every irritation, every betrayal?

He could hear their unspoken thoughts.

Was it hard for Jesus to love Peter, knowing that Peter would someday curse him? Was it tough to trust Thomas, knowing Thomas would one day question Jesus' resurrection? Just days before Jesus' death, his disciples were arguing about which of them was the best! How did Jesus resist the urge to recruit a new batch of followers? How was he able to love people who were hard to *like?*

Few things stir panic like being trapped in a relationship. It's one thing to be stuck with a puppy but something else entirely to be stuck in a family or school or friendship situation.

We might chuckle over goofy terms like *stuckititis,* but for many, this is no laughing matter. Which is why it's such a perfect way to begin our study of what it means to be just like Jesus—by examining his heart of forgiveness. How *was* Jesus able to love his disciples? The answer is found in the thirteenth chapter of John, when Jesus kneels before his disciples and washes their feet.

With Towel and Basin

It was just before the Passover Feast. Jesus knew the time had come for him to leave this world and go to the Father. But not without one more display of love . . .

It has been a long day. Jerusalem is packed with Passover guests. The spring sun is warm. The streets are dusty. A splash of cool water on tired, aching feet would be refreshing.

The disciples enter the supper room and take their places around the table. On the wall hangs a towel, and on the floor sit a pitcher and a basin. Any one of the disciples could have volunteered for the job, but not one does.

After a few moments Jesus stands and removes his outer robe. He wraps a servant's sash around his waist, takes up the basin, and kneels before one of the disciples. He unlaces a sandal and gently lifts the foot and places it in the basin, covers it with water, and begins to bathe it. One grimy foot after another, Jesus works his way down the row.

In Jesus' day the washing of feet was a task reserved not just for servants, but for the *lowest* of servants. In *this* case the one with the towel and basin is the King of the universe.

Hands that shaped the stars now wash away filth. Fingers that formed mountains now massage toes. And the one before whom all nations will one day kneel now kneels before his disciples. Hours before his own death, Jesus has one concern. He wants his disciples to know how much he loves them. More than removing dirt, Jesus is removing doubt.

You can be sure Jesus knows the future of these feet he is washing. These twenty-four feet will not spend the next day following their Master, defending his cause. These feet will dash for cover at the flash of a Roman sword. One pair won't even make it that far; Judas Iscariot will abandon him to his enemies that very night.

I looked for a Bible translation that reads, "Jesus washed all the disciples' feet except the feet of Judas," but I couldn't find one. Knowing what was to come, Jesus silently lifts the feet of Judas and washes them clean—cleansing with kindness the one who would betray him.

Behold the gift Jesus gives his followers! He knows what these men are about to do. By morning they will bury their heads in shame and look down at their feet in disgust. And when they do, he wants them to remember how he knelt before them and washed their feet. He wants them to realize those feet are still clean. "You don't understand now what I am doing, but you will understand later" (John 13:7 NCV).

Remarkable. He forgave their sin before they even committed it. He offered mercy before they even asked for it.

Jesus still cleans his disciples' feet. Jesus still washes away stains. Jesus still purifies his people. But

Because Jesus has forgiven us, we can forgive others.

that's not all he does. Because Jesus has forgiven us, we can forgive others. Because he has a forgiving heart, we can have a forgiving heart. We can have a heart like his.

> > > It was really Courtney's fault . . . the mix-up about dates. *I cannot believe she did that,* Kate fumed. *Doesn't Miss Twinkletoes know what calendars are for?!*

It was really Kate's fault . . . Courtney was convinced. *Where are Miss Organized's famous "reminders" when you really need them?!*

It was really *nobody's* fault. The scheduling of the awards banquet and the ballet recital was outside their control. Of course, it *would* have helped if Courtney had noticed that the twenty-third was *this* Friday. And it was too bad that—for once—Kate had neglected to "program" Courtney's memory.

So things were a little strained that week. And the usual traffic between Ruffle City and the House of Neat came to a halt—unlike the *thoughts* racing through two troubled minds.

The problem was, each girl knew the other too well *not* to know how important *both* Friday events were. Courtney knew how thrilled Kate was to be up for Most Valuable Player. And Kate knew how hard Courtney had worked on her featured role in Friday's recital.

Neither wanted to see the other disappointed. Neither wanted to see herself disappointed, either! So, 'round and 'round it went. Each time one girl thought of a reason why *her* event was more important, she'd think of *other* things, too.

For Kate, it was Courtney's patience teaching her the not-as-easy-as-they-look ballet exercises that gave Kate the strongest/fastest soccer legs in the league. Or Courtney's tact in pointing out really cool clothes, without ever mentioning that there was life beyond sweats.

For Courtney, it was the trouble Kate took to help her make *sense* of math. Or the way she bragged about Courtney's dancing to her soccer team-mates. Or Kate's cheerful "No problem" when Courtney showed up late . . . again.

> "Before this evening ends, there's one more presentation to be made."

It was Kate—with typical Kate logic—who made the decision. It was Courtney who made a plan of her own, and—with very *un*-typical efficiency—made it happen.

> > > > > > > > > > > >

Courtney sank into a graceful bow. It was her third curtain call. *And well deserved!* thought Kate, applauding with soccer-match enthusiasm from her front-row seat.

Courtney smiled as a piercing whistle cut through the applause. *Leave it to Kate!* An enormous bouquet (Kate's idea) cradled in one arm, Courtney rose to her feet. But rather than leave the stage, she simply stood there.

The puzzled audience grew quiet as Courtney opened her mouth.

Leave it to Courtney, thought Kate with a grin. *She's going to make a speech!*

And she did. "Before this evening ends, there's one more presentation to be made." With a sweeping gesture, Courtney cued an off-stage helper, who brought out a gleaming . . . *soccer (?!)* . . . trophy.

"To be here for *me* this evening, someone very special gave up her own moment in the spotlight." Then, with a fanfare in her voice, "Ladies and gentlemen, it's my pleasure to present Midvale Soccer League's Most Valuable Player . . . my sister, Kate!"

Oh, my. Oh, no! Oh, . . . help! Kate had no idea what to do. But—with a push from her family—she found herself, somehow, on stage.

"Courtney!"

"Kate!" mimicked her sister, with a grin and a hug. Then Courtney whispered, "They got the inscription wrong, though. It *should* read 'Most Valuable *Sister.*'"

Speechless, Kate just hugged her back. Then . . .

"Uh . . . Courtney?"

"Yes?"

"What do we do *now?*"

Courtney laughed. "We take a bow, Kate."

And—arms filled with roses and soccer trophy—they did. Together.

Mercy and a Message

Jesus washes our feet for two reasons. The first is to give us mercy; the second is to give us a message. And that message is simply this: Jesus offers unconditional grace; we are to offer unconditional grace. The mercy of Christ came before our mistakes; our mercy must come before the mistakes of others. Those in the circle of Christ had no doubts of his love; those in our circles should have no doubts about ours.

What does it mean to have a heart like his? It means to kneel as Jesus knelt, touching the grimy parts of the people we are stuck with and washing away their unkindnesses with kindness. Or as Paul wrote, "Be kind and loving to each other, and forgive each other just as God forgave you in Christ" (Ephesians 4:32 NCV).

"But, Max," you are saying, "I've done nothing wrong. I'm not the one who cheated or lied. I'm not the one with the annoying habits. I'm not the guilty party here." Perhaps you aren't. But neither was Jesus. Of all the men in that room, only one was worthy of having his feet washed. And he was the one who washed the feet. The one worthy of being served, served others. The genius of Jesus' example is that the burden of bridge-building falls on the strong one, not on the weak one. The one who is innocent is the one who makes the gesture.

And you know what happens? More often than not, if the one in the right volunteers to wash the feet of the one in the wrong, *both* parties get on their knees. Don't we all think we are right? Therefore, we all wash each other's feet.

And that's the secret: Relationships don't thrive because the guilty are punished, but because the innocent are merciful. Because the one who is hurt is the one who has the courage and grace to say, "I forgive you. I love you. Let's move on."

Just like Jesus.

4

THE TOUCH OF GOD

(A COMPASSIONATE HEART)

Since you have been chosen by God
who has given you this new kind of life,
and because of his deep love and concern
for you, you should practice tenderhearted
mercy and kindness to others.
— COLOSSIANS 3:12 TLB

> > > "No! NO-O-O-O!"

Evan's eyes snapped open and he thrashed upright in a tangle of sheets. Hands shaking, heart pounding, he was as breathless as if he had just run a mile.

With several jabs of a fumbling hand, he finally managed to silence the jangle of his industrial-strength alarm clock. *How weird! What was* that *all about?!*

Still a little fuzzy-minded, he glanced around the dawn-lit room with cautious brown eyes—Yup, *looked* like his. Then, with a shake of his head, everything snapped into focus. And he began to remember.

Wow . . . some dream! Kind of like being in a very strange movie!

May I ask you to look at your hand for a moment? Look at the back, then the palm. Say hello to your fingers. Run a thumb over your knuckles.

What if someone were to make a documentary film—tell your story—based on the life of your hands? The film would probably begin with an infant's fist, then a closeup of a tiny hand wrapped around Mommy's finger. Then what? Holding on to a chair as you learned to walk? Handling a spoon as you learned to eat?

It's not too long before we see your hand being loving; stroking Daddy's face or petting a puppy. Nor is it too long before we see your hand being mean; pushing big brother or yanking back a toy. All of us learned early that the hand is . . . handy . . . for more than just survival—it's also a tool for expressing our feelings. The same hand can help or hurt, reach out or clench tight . . . lift someone up or shove someone down.

Were you to show the film to your friends, you'd be proud of certain moments: your hand holding out a gift, folding in prayer, or reaching out with sympathy and understanding in a touch of *compassion*. And then there are the other scenes. Shots of accusing fingers, angry fists. Hands taking more often than giving, demanding instead of offering, wounding rather than loving.

Oh, the power of our hands. Leave them unmanaged and they become weapons: clawing for power, clutching with greed, grabbing for pleasure. But manage them and our hands become instruments of grace—not just tools in the hands of God, but *God's very hands*. When we seek to do God's will and not our own, our hands become his hands, doing heaven's work on earth.

That's what Jesus did. Our Savior completely surrendered his hands to God. The documentary of his hands has no scenes of greedy grabbing or unfounded finger pointing. It does, however, have scene after scene of people longing for his compassionate touch. And each one who came was touched. And each one touched was changed. But none were touched or changed more than the unnamed leper of Matthew 8.

> When Jesus came down from the hill, great crowds followed him. Then a man with a skin disease came to Jesus. The man bowed down before him and said, "Lord, you can heal me if you will."
>
> Jesus reached out his hand and touched the man and said, "I will. Be healed!" And immediately the man was healed from his disease. Then Jesus said to him, "Don't tell anyone about this. But go and show yourself to the priest and offer the gift Moses commanded for people who are made well. This will show the people what I have done."
>
> —MATTHEW 8:1–4 NCV

Mark and Luke tell this story, too. But with apologies to all three writers, I must say none tell *enough*. Oh, we know the man's disease and his decision, but as to the rest? We are left with questions. The authors offer no name, no history, no description.

The Ultimate Outcast

Sometimes my curiosity gets the best of me, and I wonder out loud. That's what I'm about to do here—wonder out loud about the man who felt Jesus' compassionate touch. He makes one appearance, has one request, and receives one touch. But that one touch changed his life forever. And I wonder if his story went something like this:

For five years no one touched me. No one. Not one person. Not my wife. Not my child. Not my friends. No one touched me. They saw me. They spoke to me. I heard love in their voices. I saw concern in their eyes. But I didn't feel their touch.

There was no touch. Not once. No one touched me.

What you take for granted, I longed for. Handshakes. Warm embraces. A tap on the shoulder to get my attention. Such moments were taken from my world. No one touched me. No one bumped into me. What I would have given to be bumped into, to be caught in a crowd, for my shoulder to brush against

> **What you take for granted, I longed for. Handshakes. Warm embraces.**

another's. But for five years it has not happened. How could it? I was not allowed on the streets. I was not permitted in my synagogue. Not even welcome in my own house.

I was untouchable. I was a leper. And no one touched me. Until today.

I wonder about this man because in New Testament times leprosy was the most dreaded disease. The condition caused the body to decay while it still lived! Leprosy was death by inches.

The social consequences were as dreadful as the physical. Considered contagious, the leper was kept apart from others, sent away to a leper colony.

In Scripture, the leper symbolizes the ultimate outcast: infected by a condition he did not seek, rejected by those he knew, avoided by everyone else, condemned to a future he could not bear. And in the memory of each outcast must have been the day he was forced to face the truth: Life would never be the same.

》 》 》 Still puzzling over The Dream (if ever one deserved capital letters, that one did!), Evan was even more on autopilot than usual. Fortunately, his morning routine required little actual brain involvement. Though he *did* notice some things seemed slightly out of whack.

Funny, I thought I just had a haircut. Why does it

look so . . . strange? And when did I buy that shirt . . . and what was I thinking?! Hey, where did that poster come from??? I can't stand that kind of mus—

"Evan . . . better hurry. You're running late!"

"Coming, Mom." Grabbing his backpack, Evan stepped into the shoes he didn't recognize and dashed for the stairs.

The messy-haired boy in the *very* strange clothes who floundered through the kitchen was as much a surprise to his family as to himself. Where was ultra-smooth, trendy Evan-the-Cool?! And *who* was that "stranger" gobbling a piece of toast and tripping down the front steps on his way to school?

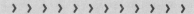

His welcome to math class—when he stumbled in, ten minutes late—was a frown from Mrs. Harris, a real stickler for being on time. But that was kind of hard to do when—for starters—you couldn't even find your own locker! (*How* had he ended up at the farthest end of the dimmest hall, *miles* away from all his friends?)

His attempt at a humorous apology hit the floor with a dull *thud.* The only laugh he got came at the blackboard, when his usually sharp mind went completely blank! And that laugh wasn't so much *with* him, as *at* him. Strange. But not as strange as the "looks" he'd been getting.

What was *wrong* with people? Kids who'd usually

go out of their way to catch his attention seemed to be . . . avoiding him. Kids who'd usually check out his gear to see what *they* wanted next, seemed to find today's choices . . . laughable. And his friends—the "with it" group he'd always hung out with—didn't seem to see him at all! Oh, sure, he'd seen *them*—always in the distance. He'd even waved and tried to catch up. But they seemed to look right through him. As if he didn't exist . . . or wasn't worth noticing.

By lunch time, he had stopped wondering what was wrong with everyone and started wondering what was wrong with *him*.

How had he become so uncool and "out of it"? *Oh, no, you don't suppose . . . ?!*

A look in the locker room mirror confirmed his worst fears. The not-quite-right clothes. The awkward, bewildered look. The doesn't-have-a-clue impression he made. It *was* true. He was definitely—maybe terminally—"*different*"!

What was going on?! Was he hallucinating? Had he stepped into a *Twilight Zone* episode? (A perfectly natural question for a sci-fi fan like Evan.) Or was he dream—

Yikes! The Dream. This is exactly like The Dream. Only it seems to be . . . happening!

What must it have been like for Jesus' leper when he first realized that life as he knew it was over?

One year during harvest my grip on the scythe seemed weak. The tips of my fingers lost feeling, first one then another. Soon I could grip the tool but scarcely felt it. By the end of the season I felt nothing at all. I said nothing to my wife, but I know she suspected something.

One afternoon I plunged my hands into a basin of water to wash. The water turned red. My finger was bleeding, badly. But I didn't even know I was wounded. I felt nothing. And it wasn't just my hand.

"It's on your clothes, too," my wife said softly from behind me. I looked down at the bloody spots on my robe. I must have had other unfelt wounds. For the longest time I stood over the basin, staring at my hand. Somehow I knew my life was being forever changed.

"Shall I go with you to tell the priest?" she asked, knowing what the law required.

"No," I sighed, "I'll go alone."

I turned and looked into her tear-filled eyes. Then I bent down and stroked our little daughter's cheek, saying nothing. What could I say? I looked again at my wife. She touched my shoulder, and with my good hand, I touched hers. It would be our last touch.

The priest didn't touch me. He looked at my hand, now wrapped in a rag. He looked at my face, now shadowed in sorrow. I've never blamed him for what he said. He was only doing as he was taught. He covered his mouth and extended his hand, palm forward. "You are unclean," he told me. With one pronouncement I lost my family, my farm, my future, my friends.

⟩ ⟩ ⟩ The clincher came at lunch. Tray in hand, Evan started for his usual table—then stopped dead in his tracks. The table was still there. So was the laughing, chattering group of friends he *always* ate with. The problem was, there was no room for *him*. And no one seemed to miss him at all!

In fact, there didn't seem to be any room for him anywhere. And always-confident Evan-the-Cool was feeling very . . . uncomfortable. It was a feeling he was starting to get used to. (It doesn't take a lot of being ignored, or laughed at, or treated as a "nobody" to make you start wondering if maybe people are right about you.)

Then he saw a hand wave, motioning him over to a table way in back. He was being invited to eat in . . . "Losers' Corner"! He'd named it himself, actually, just last week. He was only goofing off, but Kelly—usually one of his biggest fans—had really gotten on his case about it. "That's

He was being invited to eat in . . . "Losers' Corner"!

really mean, Evan! So what if they don't 'fit in'? They're still people—with feelings—just like us."

Well, not exactly *like us,* thought Evan. They were all so . . . different. And didn't they know *who* he was?! Evan-the-Cool. Evan-the-Trendsetter. Evan-the—

Come to think of it, he had a feeling today's description would be a lot less kind. And that was so bogus! He was the same guy inside . . . only the "packaging" was different. And why should *that* matter?

But apparently it did. In all that busy, noisy room, the only hand reaching out to him belonged to a kid he'd usually never even . . . notice. (It didn't exactly arrive with a clap of thunder, but it was a revelation nonetheless.)

Well, Mister Not-As-Cool-As-You-Thought, maybe it's time to find out what you've been missing.

It turned out, he'd been missing a lot. Inside those outsides that didn't quite measure up to *some* people's definition of "cool" were sharp minds and good hearts and really fascinating—if sometimes *unusual*—tastes and interests and ideas.

Not that he'd ever become a chess fanatic like Marcus, but he wouldn't mind having a brain like that. And who would have dreamed that quiet little Lita could get so excited about *baseball* of all things? Or that there were actually *classical* music fan clubs—*and* T-shirts?

Come to think of it, he probably struck them as a little "exotic," too. But then, who *says* everyone has to look and think and act exactly alike?!

On the strangest day of his life, Evan's circle had somehow grown larger—and richer. All it took was a friendly hand, reaching out, to make all the difference.

Kelly had been right to call him on labeling people before he knew them. "What if it were *you*, Evan?" she'd asked, blue eyes flashing. "How would you like being treated that way?"

As a matter of fact, *that* was the question he'd gone to sleep with last night.

The banishing of a leper seems cruel. But the Ancient East hasn't been the only culture to set apart their wounded. Oh, we might not build leper colonies or cover our mouths in their presence, but we certainly build "walls" and turn our eyes away from those who make us uncomfortable.

One of my sadder memories involves my fourth-grade friend Jerry (not his real name). He and a half-dozen of us were always together. Until the day we found out his father drank too much. For some reason—and it still makes me ashamed—that changed everything. Jerry, the second baseman; Jerry, the kid with the red bike; Jerry, my friend on the corner, was suddenly Jerry, the son of an alcoholic.

Sometimes kids can be hard, and for some reason we were hard on Jerry. He was "infected." Like the leper, he suffered from a condition he didn't create. Like the leper, he was put outside the "village."

There are many in our world who know this feeling. The "different" ones who might not look or dress or think or speak as we do. The people we perceive to be untouchables *we* create, because they make us feel so . . . uncomfortable.

And only God knows how many Jerrys are in *voluntary* exile—people living quiet, lonely lives infected by their fear of rejection and their memories of the last time they tried. They choose not to be touched at all rather than risk being hurt again.

Five years have passed, and no one has touched me since, until today. Oh, how I horrified those who saw me. Five years of leprosy had done terrible things to my body. At the sight of me, fathers grabbed their children. Mothers covered their faces. Children pointed and stared. And—always—the shouts of "Unclean! Unclean! Unclean!" I was no longer a person; I was a disease.

The rags on my body couldn't hide my sores. Nor could the wrap on my face hide the rage in my eyes . . . and heart. I didn't even try to hide it. How many nights did I shake my crippled fist at the silent sky? "What did I do to deserve this?" But never a reply.

Oh, yes, I was angry. Angry, and desperate. And I think that's what made me take the step I took today. Of course, it was risky. But what did I have to lose? He calls himself God's Son. Either he will hear my complaint and kill me or accept my demands and heal me. Those were my thoughts. I came to him as a defiant man, moved not by faith but by a desperate anger.

But then I saw him, and when I saw him, I was changed. I'm a farmer, not a poet, so I cannot find the words to describe what I saw. All I can say is that Judean mornings are sometimes so fresh and the sunrises so glorious that to look at them is to forget the heat of the day before and the hurt of times past. When I looked at his face, I saw a Judean morning.

Before he spoke, I knew he cared. Somehow I knew he hated this disease as much as—no, more than—I hate it. My rage became trust, and my anger became hope.

I waited until he was only paces away, then I stepped out.

"Master!"

He stopped and looked in my direction as did dozens of others. Fear swept across the crowd. Arms flew in front of faces. "Unclean!" someone shouted. But I scarcely noticed them. Their panic I'd seen a thousand times. His compassion, however, I'd never beheld before. Everyone stepped back except him. He stepped toward me. Toward me.

I did not move. I just spoke. "Lord, you can heal me if you will." Had he healed me with a word, I would have been thrilled. Had he cured me with a prayer, I would have rejoiced. But he wasn't satisfied with just speaking to me. He drew near me. He touched me. No one had touched me in five years. Until today.

"I will." His words were as tender as his touch. "Be healed!"

And I was. I was!

And I will never forget the one who dared to touch me. He could have healed me with a word. But he wanted to do more than heal me. He wanted to honor me, to make me "real" again, to christen me. Imagine that . . . unworthy of the touch of a man, yet worthy of the touch of God.

The Power of the Godly Touch

The touch did not heal the leper's disease, you know. Matthew is careful to mention that it was the pronouncement and not the touch of Christ that cured him.

The infection was banished by a word from Jesus.

The loneliness, however, was treated by a *touch* from Jesus.

Oh, the power of a godly touch. Haven't you known it? The doctor who treated you, or the teacher who dried your tears? A comforting hand on your shoulder during a tough time? A pastoral blessing? Haven't we all known the power of a godly touch?

Can't we offer the same? In ways large *and* small?

The answer, of course, is yes. But sometimes we tend to forget the power of a loving touch—from hand . . . or heart. We fear saying the wrong thing or using the wrong tone or acting the wrong way. So, rather than do it incorrectly, we do nothing at all.

Aren't we glad Jesus didn't make the same mistake? If

your fear of doing the wrong thing keeps you from doing anything, keep in mind the perspective of the lepers of the world. They aren't picky. They aren't finicky. They're just lonely. They are yearning for a godly touch.

Jesus touched the untouchables of the world. Will you do the same?

Jesus touched the untouchables of the world. Will you do the same?

> › › › Evan's eyes snapped open to the ignore-me-if-you-dare jangle of his alarm clock. By the time he'd jabbed it into silence, he was awake.
>
> Or was he? *Strange, I've never wondered about that before.*
>
> Even stranger was his next thought: *Well, what's it gonna be? A day to be different . . . or a day to make a difference?*
>
> *Man . . . where did that come from?*
>
> Then his eyes opened even wider, as he began to remember The Dream. (Or *was* it a dream?) Holding his breath, Evan began to look cautiously around his room . . . everything seemed to be back to normal. *It was a dream!* Then he smiled and thought: *But I'm going to make it a reality!*

5 | HEARING GOD'S MUSIC

(A LISTENING HEART)

Do not merely listen to the word, and so deceive yourselves. Do what it says. Anyone who listens to the word but does not do what it says is like a man who looks at his face in a mirror and, after looking at himself, goes away and immediately forgets what he looks like.
—JAMES 1:22–24 NIV

Let's pretend for a minute. Let's pretend you're at the concert of your dreams, with your very favorite singer or group performing. Hours of music you absolutely love, *plus*—incredible as it might seem—there's a song written just for *you!* Nothing could be more perfect, right?

Except . . . "stuff" keeps getting in the way. You get there late because you couldn't decide what to wear. And, of course, finding the "perfect" seat takes time, too. Then you get thirsty, which means a trip to the refreshment stand, where you run into some friends, and start . . . talking. And all the time you're so busy with your own concerns, the music is happening. And you don't hear *any* of it! Nada. None. Missed the whole thing!

No way, you're thinking. *No way would that happen!* Of course you'd show up on time. Of course you'd pay attention. Of course you'd listen to the music! Or would you? Have you? *Are* you?

We're not very good at it, you know. Listening. So much stuff gets in the way—as Jesus well knew. In fact, he made quite a point of reminding us how important it *is* to listen.

> > > > > > > > > > > >

More than once Jesus said, "Let he who has ears to hear, use them." Eight times in the Gospels and eight times in the book of Revelation we are reminded that it's not enough just to have ears—we must use them.

In one of his parables (Mark 4:1–20), Jesus compared our ears to soil. He told about a farmer who scattered seed (a symbol for the Word) in four different types of ground (a symbol for our ears). Some of our ears are like a hard road—can't get *anything* to grow there. Others have ears like rocky soil—we hear the Word

> "Let he who has ears to hear, use them."

but don't allow it to take root. Still others have ears much like a weed patch—too crowded, too thorny, with too much competition for the seed to have a chance. And then there are some who have ears that hear: prepared, attentive, and ready to hear God's voice.

Please note that in all four cases the seed is the same seed. The sower is the same sower. What's different is not the message or the messenger—it's the listener. And if the proportion in the story is significant, three-fourths of the world isn't listening to God's voice. Whether it's because of hard hearts, shallow lives, or distracted minds, 75 percent of us are missing the message!

It's not that we don't have ears; it's that we don't use them!

Scripture has always stressed the importance of hearing God's voice. "Happy are those who listen to me" is the promise of Proverbs 8:34 (NCV).

Our ears, unlike our eyes, do not have lids. They are meant to remain open, but how easily they close.

Mine closed in the luggage store, where I had spent quite a lot of time with a helpful clerk. When I told him I was going to another store to compare prices, he asked if I wanted to take his business card. "No," I said, "your name is easy to remember: Bob."

To which he replied, "My name is Joe."

I had heard the man, but I hadn't listened.

Pilate didn't listen, either. He had the classic case of ears that didn't hear. Not only did his wife warn him that Jesus was innocent, but the very Word of life stood before Pilate and proclaimed, "Everyone who belongs to the truth listens to me" (John 18:37 NCV). But Pilate had "selective" hearing. He allowed the voices of the people to drown out the voices of conscience and the Carpenter.

"Let he who has ears to hear, use them." How long has it been since you had your hearing checked? When God throws seed your way, what is the result? How well *do* you hear God's voice?

> > > Amanda Carter had a "hearing" problem. Oh, her ears worked just fine; it was just that what passed through them didn't always *register* on her brain. Which, a few months ago, led to a very close call.

It wasn't as if her best friend, Sara, hadn't tried—in all kinds of ways—to let her know what was going on. But Amanda had been so focused on her own concerns and her "warp-speed" schedule, that she'd missed all the clues. And because of that, she'd come close—too close—to letting Sara down in the worst possible way. She'd come close to letting God down, too. Proving once again the wisdom of that familiar parental refrain: "Amanda, learn to *listen!*"

How Long Has It Been Since You Let God Have You?

I mean really *have* you? How long since you gave him some uninterrupted time listening for his voice? Jesus did. He made an on-purpose effort to spend time with God.

Spend some time in Scripture reading about the *listening* life of Jesus, and you'll see a pattern of regular time with God. Luke tells us, "Jesus often withdrew to lonely places and prayed" (Luke 5:16 NIV).

Ready for a no-brainer of a "test" question? *If Jesus, the Son of God, the sinless Savior of humankind, thought it important to clear his calendar to pray, wouldn't we be wise to do the same?*

Not only did he spend regular time with God in prayer, he spent regular time in God's Word. Of course, we don't find Jesus pulling a leather-bound New Testament from his satchel and reading it. We do, however, see the stunning example of Jesus, tempted in the wilderness, using the Word of God to deal with Satan. Three times he is tempted, and each time he repels the attack with the phrase: "It is written in the Scriptures" (Luke 4:4, 8, 12 NCV), and then he quotes a verse.

Jesus is so familiar with Scripture that he not only knows the verse, he knows how to *use* it!

And then there's the time when Jesus was asked to read in the synagogue. He is handed the book of Isaiah the prophet. He finds the passage, reads it, and declares, "While you heard these words just now, they were coming true!" (Luke 4:21 NCV). We are shown the picture of a person who knows his way around in Scripture *and* can recognize its fulfillment!

And here's another "test" question. *If Jesus thought it wise to grow familiar with the Bible, shouldn't we do the same?*

If we are to be just like Jesus—if we are to have ears that hear God's voice—then we have just found two habits worth imitating: the habits of prayer and Bible reading.

> > > Amanda lived life on the run. If she wasn't chairing a class or club meeting, she was practicing piano or gymnastics, or spearheading a fund-raiser, or hitting the books to keep up her straight-A grades, or saving the environment, or . . .

Well, you get the picture.

And, the thing was, she was really great at all of it. She was efficient. ("How can one person accomplish so *much?!*") She was inspiring. ("A born leader!") She was organized. ("She's already picked out her college *and* medical school!") When Amanda took charge, things got *done!*

Most people got tired even *watching* Amanda zip around. The only one who came anywhere close to keeping up with her was Sara. She'd been Amanda's "partner-in-crime"—and very best friend—since second grade. For friendship's sake, Sara stretched herself to the limit to share in at least some of Amanda's projects. Until a few months ago, that is.

Amanda didn't notice at first that she was seeing less and less of Sara. She also didn't notice, when Sara did show up, that she wasn't the same light-hearted "old" Sara. Gone was the infectious giggle. Gone were the energy and enthusiasm. Gone were

Sara's playful attempts to slow down Amanda's frantic pace: "Hold it there, Flash, you're dealing with mere mortals here!"

Even her mom's concerned question didn't set off any alarms for Amanda: "What's up with Sara, Mandy? She seemed a little down the last time she was here."

"Oh, she's fine, Mom. You know Sara, she can deal with anything. Besides, she'd tell me if there was a *real* problem."

Amanda's mom didn't look very convinced. "Sometimes we have to listen for *more* than words. People tell us things in lots of ways. You know, Amanda, a friend is a precious *gift* . . . and God expects us to take good care of his gifts." But before she could say anything more, Amanda was out the door.

"Gymnastics . . . gotta run, Mom!"

Yes, there were plenty of clues. But it took a long time for Amanda to even begin to wonder if something was wrong. Even when Sara finally did try to *talk* about her troubles—something she rarely did—things kept getting in the way. It wasn't that Amanda didn't have time for her friend; she just didn't have time right *now*.

When Sara called Tuesday night, it was: "Could you see what she wants, Mom? I've *got* to finish this report."

When Sara—who'd arrived *very* late—caught up with Amanda after youth group, it was: "Gotta run, Sara. But Kim can fill you in on the fund-raiser."

When Sara suggested lunch on Saturday "to catch up on things," it was: "Sounds like fun, but I'm really snowed right now. Maybe Molly or Karen would like to— Sara! Is something wrong?"

There was no easy answer to that question. Sara didn't even try for one. She just stood there, her big blue eyes overflowing with tears. Suddenly—and finally!—all the pieces snapped into place in Amanda's mind. *Of course there's something wrong! How could I have missed it?!* Amanda—the master organizer, achiever, delegator—was face to face with one of those moments when there is absolutely *no* substitute for a loving— listening—*friend.*

Sara . . . just stood there, her big blue eyes overflowing with tears.

Substitute Spirituality

If we are to be just like Jesus, we must have a regular time of talking to God and listening to his Word.

Wait a minute. Don't you do that. I know exactly what some of you are doing. You are tuning me out. You're thinking: *Max is talking about daily devotionals, eh? This is a good time for me to take a mental walk over to the fridge and see what we have to eat.*

I understand your foot-dragging. Some of us have tried to

have a daily quiet time, and it hasn't worked out all that well. Others of us have a hard time concentrating—too many distractions. And *all* of us are busy. So rather than spend time with God, listening for his voice, we'll let others spend time with him and then benefit from their experience. Let *them* tell us what God is saying. After all, isn't that why we pay preachers? Isn't that why we read Christian books? *These folks are good at daily devotionals. I'll just learn from them.*

Is that *your* approach? Are your spiritual experiences secondhand? If they are, here's a question for you: Do you do that with other parts of your life? I don't think so.

You don't do that with vacations. You don't say, "Visiting a theme park is such a hassle; packing bags, traveling, waiting in line for every ride. I'm going to send someone for me. When he gets back, I'll hear all about it and save myself all the trouble."

Would you do that? No! You want to experience every sight, every sound, every stomach-clenching, heart-stopping, spin-twist-plunge of every ride, firsthand. Some things no one can do for you.

Or what about finally getting a chance to spend time with that "certain someone" you'd like to know better? Are you going to send a substitute to the mall or movies or skate park to enjoy the pleasure of his or her company? Not on your life! Certain things no one can do for you.

You don't let someone eat on your behalf, do you? You don't say, "Chewing is such a bother; my jaws get too tired, and all those different tastes are *so* confusing. I'm going to hire someone to chew my food, and I'll just swallow whatever he gives me." Would you do that? Yuck! Of course not! Certain things no one can do for you.

And one of those is spending time with God.

Listening to God is a firsthand experience. When he asks for your attention, God doesn't want you to send a substitute; he wants you. He wants *you* to vacation in his splendor. He invites *you* to feel the touch of his hand. He invites *you* to feast at his table. He wants to spend time with *you*. And—with a little practice and the right tools—your time with God can be the highlight of your day.

Wait a minute! Practice I understand, but "tools"?! What tools? I don't have any tools!

Oh, yes, you do . . . all you have to do is *use* them.

> ❯ ❯ ❯ Seeing her friend in tears was a real wake-up call for Amanda. Sara *never* cried! Most things just bounced off the little blonde with the sunny outlook on life. When clouds *did* gather in Sara's world, she'd always liked to work things out for herself.
>
> But not this time. *This* time, Sara couldn't seem to cope at all!
>
> *Well, that's what friends are for, isn't it?!* Without a second thought, Amanda threw her precious "schedule" out the window and put her arm around Sara's shoulders.
>
> "Sara, tell me what's going on." And this time, Amanda listened—*really* listened—with her ears, with her eyes, with her heart.

What she heard made her almost as sad as Sara. Her best friend's fun, funny, *adorable* parents were talking about divorce! *Why that's, that's . . .*

"So . . . awful," said Sara, finishing Amanda's thought.

What she heard made her almost as sad as Sara.

"Oh, they *say* they're try- ing to work things out. And they're seeing a family counselor. But they both seem so . . . angry all the time. *Nothing's* the same, Mandy. Nothing! I've prayed about it. And I *know* God doesn't make mistakes. But I still feel like the ground cracked open under my feet. And I don't know what to d-d-do."

As the story poured out, Amanda made a startling discovery. Listening, never her strength, wasn't all that hard after all—if you stopped looking ahead and con- centrated on *now* . . . and if you *cared.* And, oh, did she care!

Amanda wasn't sure exactly what to say when Sara finally wound down. But, blessedly, she did say exactly the right thing. "I'm so sorry, Sara. Sorry for what's happening. Sorry I haven't been much of a friend when you really needed one."

"Well . . . ," Sara graciously offered with a watery smile, "I *could* have said something."

"No," said Amanda, "*I* should have been paying attention. It's that 'listening' thing my folks are always going on about. You might have noticed I'm not very good at it?" (*That* actually got a grin from Sara.)

"But," said Amanda, grinning back, "that doesn't mean I can't get better . . . and I will!" That settled, Amanda put her busy brain to work on Sara's problem.

"You're right, Sara, God doesn't make mistakes," she said. Then, with a definite gleam in her eye, "But I'll bet he doesn't mind a little human help now and then to get things moving in the right direction . . ."

Sara was looking less tragic by the moment. Her problem was still there, and still as big as ever. The difference was, she wasn't alone with it any longer.

"Uh-oh." Amanda suddenly had the strangest look on her face as she remembered *who* else she hadn't been listening to!

Learning to Listen

With the right tools, we can learn to listen to God. What are these tools? Here are three I have found helpful.

1. A regular time and place. Pick a slot in your schedule and a corner of your world, and claim it for God. It might be early in the day. It might be late in the day. Or it might be several times throughout the day.

Some sit under a tree, others in the kitchen. Maybe lunch break or study period or just before bed could work for you. The important thing is to find a time and a place that are right for you.

How much time should you take? As much as you need—to say what you want and for God to say what he wants. Which leads us to your second tool . . .

2. An open Bible. God speaks to us through his Word. The first step in reading the Bible is to ask God to help you understand it. "But the Helper will teach you everything and will cause you to remember all that I told you. This Helper is the Holy Spirit whom the Father will send in my name" (John 14:26 NCV).

Before reading the Bible, pray. Don't go to Scripture looking for your own idea; go searching for God's. Read the Bible prayerfully. Also, read the Bible carefully. The Bible is not a newspaper to be skimmed but rather a mine to be quarried. "Search for it like silver, and hunt for it like hidden treasure. Then you will understand respect for the LORD, and you will find that you know God" (Proverbs 2:4–5 NCV).

And here's a practical tip. Study the Bible a little at a time. God seems to send messages as he did his manna in the desert: one day's portion at a time. Read until a verse "hits" you, then stop and think about it. Copy the verse onto paper, or write it in your journal, and reflect on it several times.

Don't be discouraged if your reading reaps a small harvest. Some days a lesser portion is all we need. A little girl returned from her first day at school. Her mom asked, "Did you learn anything?" "I guess not," the girl replied. "I have to go back tomorrow and the next day and the next day. . . ."

Such is the case with learning. And such is the case with

Bible study. Understanding comes a little at a time over a life-time. And that's where your *third* tool comes in handy . . .

3. A listening heart. We know we are listening to God when what we read in the Bible is what others see in our lives. Maybe you've heard the story of the not-so-bright fellow who saw a sign advertising a cruise for just $100 cash.

I've got a hundred dollars, he thought. *And I'd like to go on a cruise.* So he walked in and signed up. As he was count-ing out his money, he was whacked over the head and knocked out cold. He woke up in a barrel floating down a river. Another sucker in another barrel floated past and asked him, "Say, do they serve lunch on this cruise?"

The not-so-bright guy answered, "They didn't last year."

It's one thing not to know. It's another to *know* and not *learn*—to "get the message" and not *use* it! As Paul advised, "What you have learned and received and heard and seen in me, do" (Philippians 4:9 RSV).

If you want to be just like Jesus, let God have you. Spend time listening for him until you receive your lesson for the day—then *use* it.

> › › › "Be careful, Amanda," her mother said that evening, as she listened to some very elaborate schemes to get Sara's parents back together. "Family problems are a delicate thing. There are times when a friend can help, and there are times when all you can do is *be* a friend."

"But how do you *know* which is which? How do you know *what* you should do?" asked a frustrated Amanda, whose answer to everything was action.

"Well," said her mother, "you *could* ask God. Of course, to hear his answer you'd actually have to lis—"

"Listen," Amanda finished for her. "Not exactly my strong point, is it? Besides, that's the *other* problem."

"Oh?" Amanda's mom was looking a little confused. Amanda was looking a little ashamed.

"Well, you see, Mom, Sara isn't the only one I've been too busy for lately. It suddenly hit me today that I've kinda dropped out on *God*, too."

"Oh," said her mother again—just before she smiled, and absolutely stunned Amanda with her next words. "Well, I'll bet he's missed you."

What?!

"Don't look so surprised, sweetie. How could he *not* miss you? He loves you."

How Long Since You Let God Love You?

My daughters are too old for this now, but when they were young—diaper-size—I would come home, shout their names, and watch them run to me with lifted arms and squealing voices. For the next few minutes we would speak the language of love. We'd roll on the floor, gobble bellies, tickle tummies, and laugh and play.

We delighted in each other's presence. They made no requests of me, with the exception of "Let's play, Daddy." And

I made no demands of them, except, "Don't hit Daddy with the hammer."

My kids let me love them.

But suppose my daughters had come to me as we often come to God. "Hey, Dad, glad you're home. Here is what I want. More toys. More candy. And can we go to Disneyland this summer?"

"Whoa," I would have wanted to say. "I'm not a waiter, and this isn't a restaurant. I'm your father, and this is our house. Just let me tell you how much I love you."

Ever thought God might want to do the same with you? *Oh, he wouldn't say that to me.* He wouldn't? Then to whom was he speaking when he said, "I have loved you with an everlasting love" (Jeremiah 31:3 NIV)? And look at this jewel of a promise:

> The LORD your God is with you;
>> the mighty One will save you.
> He will rejoice over you.
>> You will rest in his love;
>> he will sing and be joyful about you.
>> —ZEPHANIAH 3:17 NCV

Don't move too quickly through that verse. Read it again and prepare yourself for a surprise.

Note who is *doing* something and who is *letting* something happen. Who is singing, and who is resting? Who is rejoicing over his loved one, and who is being rejoiced over?

We tend to think we are the singers and God is the

"singee." And that *is* often the case. But apparently there are times when God wishes we would just be still and (what a stunning thought!) let him sing over us.

I can see you squirming. You say you aren't worthy of such affection? Neither was Judas, but Jesus washed his feet. Neither was Peter, but Jesus fixed him breakfast.

Besides, who are we to decide if we are worthy? Our job is simply to be still long enough to let God have us and let him love us. Our job is to *listen* so we don't miss a moment, or a note, of the music God "sings" for us.

Jesus told us how: "Let the man who has ears to hear, use them."

> A regular time and place.
> An open Bible.
> An open heart.

Let God have you, and let God love you—and don't be surprised if your heart begins to hear music you've never heard before. God is singing *your* song. Are you listening?

6 | BEING LED BY AN UNSEEN HAND

(A GOD-BRIGHTENED HEART)

*I will be in them and you will
be in me so that they will be
completely one. Then the world
will know that you sent me and
that you loved them just as much
as you loved me.*
> —JOHN 17:23 NCV

〉 〉 〉 Put the ball in Rob's hands, point him toward the basket, then stand clear! Nobody worked harder to win. Nobody played a smarter, faster game. Nobody played a *fairer* game, either. Rob had even been known to call fouls on *himself!* In fact, he just did—in the biggest game of the season.

"Are you *nuts,* Rob?!" Kevin demanded. "The ref didn't see. Nobody knew!"

"Not quite true, Kevin . . . *I* knew."

"Man, for a guy who likes to win as much as you do, you sure go about it in a strange way. What's up?"

Rob grinned. "Just something my dad said once about winning."

"Just something my dad said once." It wasn't at all that unusual a statement—until you remembered that Rob's dad died when Rob was still a baby! But it wasn't really all that strange, either—if you knew Rob, and knew about the letters.

Rob had even been known to call fouls on himself!

True: It wasn't your *average* father-son relationship. But Rob and his dad still made quite a team.

It's a wonderful day indeed when we stop working *for* God and begin working *with* God. (Go ahead, read the sentence again.)

For years I viewed God as a kindly "boss" and my role as his loyal sales representative. He had his office, and I, as a minister, had my "territory." I could contact him as much as I wanted. He was always a phone or fax away. He encouraged me, stood behind me, and supported me, but he didn't go with me. At least I didn't think he did.

Then I read 2 Corinthians 6:1: We are "God's fellow workers" (NIV).

Fellow workers? Co-laborers? God and I work *together?* Imagine the shift in thinking that this truth creates. Rather than report to God, we work *with* God. Rather than check in with him and leave, we check in with him and then follow. We are always in the presence of God. We never leave church. There is never a nonsacred moment! His presence never fades away. Oh, we might not always be *aware* of his presence, but he is *always* there.

God and I work together?

This leads me to a great question: If God is always present, is it possible to enjoy nonstop communication with him? In the last chapter we talked about the importance of setting aside time every day to spend with God. Let's take the thought a step further. A giant step further. What if our daily "togetherness" *never* stopped? Would it be possible to live— *minute by minute*—in the presence of God? Is such closeness even possible? One man who wrestled with these questions wrote:

> Can we have contact with God all the time? All the time awake, fall asleep in His arms, and awaken in His presence? Can we attain that? Can we do His will all the time? Can we think His thoughts all the time? . . . Can I bring the Lord back in my mind-flow every few seconds so that God shall always be in my mind? I choose to make the rest of my life an experiment in

answering this question. (See *Practicing His Presence*, Goleta, Calif.: Christian Books, 1973.)

His name was Frank Laubach, and he was a dedicated missionary to the illiterate—teaching them to read so they could know the beauty of the Scriptures. What impresses me about this man, however, is not his teaching—it's his *listening*, as he tried to live in "continuous inner conversation with God."

He left behind an amazing journal about his constant communication with God. This time with God helped him know God better and grow closer to his heavenly Father. His experience, told in his journal, has encouraged me to try to do the same. Someday—when you're older—you, too, might like to read about his spiritual experience. And taste, as he did, the joy and wonder of "being led by an unseen hand" as he worked toward his goal of unbroken communication with God.

Was his goal realistic? *Is* this something that "ordinary" people can do? Well, you'll get a lot of different answers to those questions. But one thing everyone can agree on is that *Jesus* had this kind of constant closeness with his Father. And if we are to be just like Jesus, you and I will at least *strive* to do the same. That is, after all, what really matters . . . the *trying*.

> › › › There was a "Dad" letter for every birthday (and some in between). At first, when Rob was very small, his mother read them to him. Later, of course, the Birthday Letters were Rob's alone, to read and share as he chose.

The letters had been left in his mother's keeping, and written by his father during the months before his death from cancer. They were Rob's "connection" to the funny, sharp, *quirky* father he didn't remember . . . but *knew* as well as he knew himself.

"Boy, this 'dying thing' really stinks, Rob—leaving you and your beautiful mom. I always planned to be around forever, or at least until I'd thoroughly messed up your life. But God had other plans. And he did give me time. Time to know you and love you for a year. Time to think of all the things I'd like to tell you . . . at the right times.

"So that's the Bad News/Good News, son: I can't be there in person, but you're still stuck with your not-so-old dad. . . ."

And so the conversation began. When Rob was little, it was mostly words of encouragement about things his dad couldn't be there to help him with.

"Skinned knees are the 'price' of mastering bikes and skateboards, Rob. Racing with the wind is the reward."

So Rob would gulp back the tears and get right back on whatever he'd just fallen from.

"Never be afraid to try, son. Nobody is great at sports or arithmetic—or life—right off the bat. Just

keep your eye on the ball, throw your heart into the game . . . and have fun!"

So Rob met every new experience with grace, gumption . . . and a grin.

"People come in all kinds of 'flavors,' Rob. If you only get to know the ones who are just like you, you're going to miss some of God's most interesting work."

So Rob's circle of friends grew as he grew—and crossed all kinds of "lines" that usually keep people apart.

The content of the letters "grew" with Rob, too—keeping pace with the pains and puzzlements of growing up. And because his dad saw life as some kind of grand adventure *("You just never know what's waiting 'round the next corner")*, Rob did, too. And he welcomed whatever came along with open arms . . . and heart.

None of which cut any ice *at all* with Kevin, sitting on the Falcons' bench beside Rob—waiting to get back in the hard-fought basketball game. Correction: Kevin was doing more bouncing and fuming than sitting.

"Did you see that, Rob?! Another foul that nobody caught! Man, those Hillside guys play *dirty!"*

"So that gives us a license to do the same?" Rob raised an eyebrow at his indignant friend.

"No, I guess not," sighed Kevin. "But I sure hope we

don't need those two points you 'volunteered' to give away. Are you sure you know what you're doing, Rob?"

Rob grinned. "Not always. But I generally know *why* I'm doing it."

God's Translator

Jesus' relationship with God went far deeper than a daily appointment. Our Savior was *always* aware of his Father's presence. Listen to his words:

> The Son can do nothing on his own, but only what he sees the Father doing; for whatever the Father does, the Son does likewise.
>
> —JOHN 5:19 NRSV

Clearly, Jesus didn't act unless he saw his Father act. He didn't judge until he heard his Father judge. No act or deed occurred without his Father's guidance. His words have the ring of a translator.

There were a few times in Brazil when *I* served as a translator for an English speaker. He stood before his Brazilian audience, with the message. I stood at his side, with the language. My job was to communicate his story to the listeners. I did my best to allow his words to come *through* me. I was not free to add or subtract anything. When the speaker gestured, I gestured. As his volume increased, so did mine. When he got quiet, I did, too.

When he walked this earth, Jesus was "translating" God all the time. When God got louder, Jesus got louder. When God gestured, Jesus gestured. He was so in sync with the Father that he could declare, "I am in the Father and the Father is in me" (John 14:11 NRSV). It was as if he heard a voice others were missing.

I witnessed something similar to this on an airplane once. I kept hearing outbursts of laughter. The flight was bumpy and uncomfortable, hardly a reason for humor. But some fellow behind me was cracking up. No one else, just him. Finally, I turned to see what was so funny. He was wearing headphones and apparently listening to a comedian. Because he could hear what I couldn't, he acted differently than I did.

The same was true of Jesus. Because he could hear what others couldn't, he acted differently than they did. Remember when everyone was troubled about the man born blind? Jesus wasn't. Somehow he knew the blindness would reveal God's power (John 9:3 NCV). Remember when everyone was upset about Lazarus's illness? Jesus wasn't. Rather than hurry to his friend's bedside, he said, "This sickness will not end in death. It is for the glory of God, to bring glory to the Son of God" (John 11:4 NCV). It was as if Jesus could hear what no one else could. Jesus was constantly "tuned in" to his Father.

Do you suppose the Father wants the same for us? Absolutely. We are part of God's plan . . . the people of whom Paul says, "God knew them before he made the world. And God decided that they would be like his Son. . . ." (Romans 8:29 ICB).

Let me remind you again: God loves you just the way you are, but he refuses to leave you that way. He wants you to be just like Jesus. God wants the same constant "connection" with you that he had with his Son.

> > > Through the years—and through the letters—Rob came to know his dad rather well. In fact, it seemed as though his father was always with him. Things his dad said in the letters would pop into his mind at the oddest (and sometimes not-so-convenient) moments.

Face it, what kid with a foolproof opportunity to cheat on a test he hadn't studied for really *wants* to think about something like . . . honor? But there it was:

"Honor, Rob. Yeah, you're probably thinking it went out of style about the time King Arthur hung up his sword, right? Wrong! Honor—doing the right thing instead of the easy thing—is what keeps us on the side of the angels. It's also what lets you look in the mirror and like who you see."

Rob was never quite sure what he'd find in the letters (*". . . not really 'advice,' Rob. More like stuff I've learned—or got banged up by"*). But his dad's off-the-wall—but very *on*-target—"take" on things usually hit the nail right on the head. And a guy dealing with the challenges of eighth grade, *and* trying to figure out who he was, would take all the help he could get!

Like with women (of *all* ages), for instance:

"Beautiful, mysterious, independent creatures, Rob. They are very hard to figure out! But you don't have to understand them to admire, respect, and cherish them."

Or "easy answers":

"Sorry, kid, not a lot of those. Life is messy, Rob, and people are complicated, so all you can do is ask yourself what's the right thing—then give it your best shot."

Or that biggie, responsibility:

"Here's the bad news, kid: The buck stops with YOU! You are the one responsible for the choices you make, the things you do—which does save a lot of time otherwise wasted thinking up alibis."

"The buck stops with YOU! . . ."

Not that his dad had *all* the answers.

"Give me a break here, Rob. I'm only twenty-nine! If I'd lived longer I'd be a lot smarter by now. But there's one place you can always find true wisdom."

And there it came again—somewhere in every letter—the reminder that Rob had *another* Father, too, one who was *always* there for him. Rob's dad couldn't make the journey with him, but he'd left him a map and a compass.

"I'm not the only one who left messages for you, son. God did, too. And his messages are as close as your friendly neighborhood Bible. Spend a little time there every day and invite God into your life."

Pictures of "Connection"

In Scripture, God draws several pictures of the kind of relationship he has in mind. One is of a vine and a branch.

I am the vine, and you are the branches. If any remain in me and I remain in them, they produce much fruit. But without me they can do nothing. . . . If you remain in me and follow my teachings, you can ask anything you want, and it will be given to you.

—JOHN 15:5, 7 NCV

God wants to be as close to us as a branch is to a vine. Each is part of the other—impossible to tell where one starts and the other ends. And the branch isn't connected only at the moment of bearing fruit. No, the branch constantly draws its life from the vine.

God also uses the Temple as an example of the closeness he wants with us. "Don't you know," Paul writes, "that your body is the Temple of the Holy Spirit, who lives in you and who was given to you by God?" (1 Corinthians 6:19 TEV). Let's think about that for a moment. Was God a visitor or a resident in Solomon's Temple? Would you describe his presence as occasional or permanent? You know the answer. God didn't come and go, appear and disappear. He was a permanent presence, always available.

We are NEVER away from God . . . not even for a moment!

What incredibly good news for us! We are NEVER away from God! He is NEVER away from us—not even for a moment! God doesn't come to us on Sunday mornings and then exit on Sunday afternoons. He remains within us, always present in our lives.

Scripture uses marriage as the third example of this encouraging truth. Aren't we the bride of Christ (Revelation 21:2 NCV)? Haven't we made promises to him, and hasn't he made promises to us?

What does our marriage to Jesus say about his desire to be close to us? For one thing, the communication never stops.

In healthy marriages there is a tenderness, an honesty, an ongoing communication. The same is true in our relationship with God. Sometimes we go to him with our joys, and sometimes we go with our hurts, but we always go. As we go, the more we go, the more we become like him. Paul says we are being changed from "glory to glory" (2 Corinthians 3:18 KJV).

After a while, people who live long lives together begin to sound alike, to talk alike, even to think alike. As we walk with

God, we take on his thoughts, his principles, his attitudes. We take on his heart.

Can we take a look at one last comparison from the Bible? How about the sheep and the shepherd? Many times Scripture calls us the flock of God. We needn't know much about sheep to know that the shepherd never leaves the flock. If we see a flock coming down the path, we know a shepherd is nearby. If we see a Christian ahead, we can know the same. The Good Shepherd never leaves his sheep. "Even if I walk through a very dark valley, I will not be afraid, because you are with me" (Psalm 23:4 NCV).

God is as near to you as the vine is to the branch, as present within you as God was in the Temple, as close with you as a husband with a wife, and as devoted to you as a shepherd to his sheep.

Here is how King David described the beautiful closeness of the relationship:

I'm an open book to you; even from a distance, you
    know what I'm thinking.
You know when I leave and when I get back;
    I'm never out of your sight.
You know everything I'm going to say before I start
    the first sentence.
I look behind me and you're there, then up ahead
    and you're there, too—your reassuring presence,
    coming and going.
This is too much, too wonderful—I can't take it all in!
    —PSALM 139:1–6 MSG

Does constant communion with God seem a little overwhelming to you? Are you thinking, *Life is complicated enough. Why add this?* If so, remind yourself that God is the burden-remover, not the burden-giver. God intends for unceasing prayer to lighten—not heighten—our load.

The more we search the Bible, the more we realize that unbroken union with God is the intent and not the exception. Which means . . .

Within the reach of every Christian—within your reach—is the unending presence of God!

> › › › Not *all* the things Rob had learned from his dad's letters were, of course, exactly *comfortable* to live with. Doing the right thing, for instance.

"It's only fair to warn you, son . . . the right thing isn't always going to be the popular thing. There'll be times when you'll just have to suck it up and take your lumps."

There were probably going to be some "lumps" today—because even Rob's amazing last-second basket was not . . . quite . . . enough. Archrival Hillside beat the Falcons by two points—two points that were the price of Rob's self-confessed foul!

Oh, boy, thought Rob. Then, *Dad said there'd be days like this.* Rob squared his shoulders and started across the gym floor.

"Uh, Rob?" That was Kevin, trudging loyally by his side. "What exactly *did* your dad say about winning?"

Rob looked at the scoreboard with a rueful grin. "That the score only tells *part* of the story. What really counts is *how* you play the game."

"How you play?"

"Sure," said Rob, quoting his dad, "'Play hard. Play smart. Play fair. Winning by breaking the rules isn't winning at all.'"

〉 〉 〉 〉 〉 〉 〉 〉 〉 〉 〉 〉

Up in the bleachers Rob's mother smiled as she watched her tall son lead his team across the court to congratulate the other team.

"Rob's a lot like his father, isn't he?" said her brother, watching with her.

"Yes," she answered, blinking away a stray tear. "Yes, he is. Just like his father."

Practicing the Presence

How, then, *do* I live in God's presence? How do I detect his unseen hand on my shoulder and his quiet voice in my ear? A sheep grows familiar with the voice of the shepherd. How can you and I grow familiar with the voice of God? Here are four ideas:

1. Give God your waking thoughts. Before you face the day, face the Father. Before you step out of bed, step into his presence. I have a friend who makes it a habit to roll out of bed onto his knees and begin his day in prayer.

Personally, I don't get that far. With my head still on the pillow and my eyes still closed, I offer God the first seconds of my day. It's not a long prayer and far from formal. Depending on how much sleep I got, it might not even make sense to anyone but God. Often it's nothing more than "Thank you for a night's rest. I belong to you today."

The words themselves don't matter. It's the *thought* that counts.

Here is how the psalmist began his day: "Every morning, I tell you what I need, and I wait for your answer" (Psalm 5:3 NCV). Which leads to the second idea:

2. Give God your waiting thoughts. Spend time with him in silence. Married couples and longtime friends know the treasure of shared silence; they don't need to fill the air with constant chatter. Just being together is enough. Try being silent with God. "Be still, and know that I am God" (Psalm 46:10 NIV). Awareness of God is the fruit of stillness before God.

In his book *Finding God in Unexpected Places*, Philip Yancey writes that newscaster Dan Rather once asked Mother Teresa, "What do you say to God when you pray?"

Mother Teresa answered quietly, "I listen."

Not sure what to make of this, Rather tried again. "Well, then, what does God say?"

Mother Teresa smiled. "He listens." Which brings us to the third idea:

3. Give God your whispering thoughts. Through the centuries Christians have learned the value of brief prayers that can be whispered anywhere, in any setting. Things like, "Is this what you want me to do, God?" or "Does this please you, Lord?"

Imagine considering *every* moment an opportunity to speak with God. Your life will be filled with many such moments. Don't think so? Just check out these "statistics" I came across in Charles R. Swindoll's book *The Finishing Touch*.

By the time your life is over, you will have spent six months at stoplights, eight months opening junk mail, a year and a half looking for lost stuff (double that number in my case), and a whopping five years standing in various lines. Why don't you give these moments to God?

By giving God your whispering thoughts, the common becomes uncommon. Simple phrases such as "Thank you, Father," "You are my resting place, Jesus" can turn a bus ride into a pilgrimage. You needn't leave your classroom or kneel down in the cafeteria. Just pray where you are. Let the cafeteria become a cathedral or the classroom a chapel. Give God your whispering thoughts.

4. Give God your closing thoughts. At the end of the day, let your mind settle on him. Finish the day as you began it: talking to God. Thank him for the good parts. Question him about the hard parts. Seek his mercy. Seek his strength. And as you close your eyes, take comfort in the promise: "He who watches over Israel will neither slumber nor sleep" (Psalm 121:4 NIV).

And if you fall asleep as you pray, don't worry. What better place to doze off than in the arms of your Father?

> > > *"Inside out, Rob, that's the way God sees things, from the inside out. You can trust him with your deepest thoughts and toughest questions. You can talk to him any time, any place, anywhere."*

Rob smiled as he tucked the tattered letter back inside his Bible. Then he turned off the light and rolled over.

Thank you, Father, for letting me know my dad.

7

A CHANGED FACE AND A SET OF WINGS

(A WILLING HEART)

Our faces, then, are not covered. We all show the Lord's glory, and we are being changed to be like him. This change in us brings ever greater glory, which comes from the Lord, who is the Spirit.
—2 CORINTHIANS 3:18 NCV

Sunlight poured from his face.
—MATTHEW 17:2 MSG

› › › The Tranhs' journey here from halfway around the world had been neither quick nor easy. Leaving everything you have . . . everything you *know* . . .

never is. But that was the price of their chance for a better life, and they'd paid it gladly.

For the Tranh family, America truly was a land of endless promise. The only question was: *Which* promises would come true for *them*?

Song never had any doubt they *all* would. Her older brother, Vinh, wasn't so sure, so his American "journey" was somewhat different from hers.

People on a plane and people on a pew have a lot in common. All are on a journey. Some doze, and others gaze out the window. Most, if not all, are satisfied if what they *expect* to happen, happens.

For many, the mark of a good flight and the mark of a good worship assembly are the same. "Nice," we like to say. "It was a nice flight. It was a nice worship service." We exit the same way we enter, and we're happy to return the next time.

A few, however, are not content with nice. They long for something *more*. Many years ago I shared a flight with a little boy who proved this point. I heard him before I saw him. "Will they let me meet the pilot?" He was either lucky or clever because he made the request just as he entered the plane. The question floated into the cockpit, causing the pilot to lean out.

"Someone looking for me?" he asked.

The boy's hand flew up like he was answering his second-grade teacher's question. "I am!"

"Well, here I am."

With a nod from his mom, the youngster entered the

mysteries of the cockpit and came out minutes later with eyes wide. "Wow!" he exclaimed. "I'm so glad to be on this plane!"

No one else's face showed such wonder. I know. I looked. But I found no enthusiasm like the boy's in the faces of the other passengers. I mostly saw contentment: travelers content to be on the plane, content to sit and stare and say little.

And since that is what we were looking for, that is what we got. The boy, on the other hand, wanted more. He wanted to see the pilot. If asked to describe the flight, he wouldn't say "nice." He'd probably whip out the plastic wings the pilot gave him and say, "I saw the man up front!"

Do you see why I say people on a plane and people on a pew have a lot in common?

Enter a church sanctuary and look at the faces. A few are giggly, a couple are cranky, but by and large we are content. Content to be there. Content to sit and look straight ahead and leave when the service is over. Content to enjoy an assembly with no surprises or unexpected "bumps." "Seek and you will find," Jesus promised (Matthew 7:7 NIV). And since a nice service is what we seek, a nice service is usually what we find.

A few, however, seek more. A few come with the hopeful enthusiasm of the boy. Their minds are open. Their spirits are eager. Their hearts are willing. And those few leave as the boy did, wide-eyed with the wonder of having stood in the presence of the pilot himself.

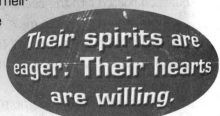

Their spirits are eager. Their hearts are willing.

> > > When five-year-old Song Tranh and her seven-year-old brother arrived in America eight years ago, their English was far from perfect. So the words "what you see is what you get" would have meant absolutely nothing to them. The *idea,* however, was something that Song seemed to have been born knowing . . . and something that Vinh never quite "got."

When people took a second look at her golden skin and tilted eyes—or smiled at her not-so-good English—Song saw it as friendly interest in *her.* So she smiled back and chattered away cheerfully (if not always understandably) in the new language that soon tasted less and less strange in her mouth.

For Vinh, though, the looks and grins (and yes, sometimes teasing) told a different story. Up went the defenses, down came the shutters, and away went the warm smile and outgoing personality that *could* have made him a lot of friends.

And not much changed in the years between then and now. Song charmed, and Vinh bristled. She collected new friends and experiences with wide-eyed delight and an infectious giggle. His wary eyes and stubborn chin made it clear that *he* was here under protest!

They both were top-of-the-class students. To disgrace their parents by being anything less—to waste this wonderful *opportunity*—was unthinkable!

They both worked hard, too, after school, to help make a success of the restaurant their parents had started. Song's sparkling eyes and tongue-in-cheek "explanations" of the more puzzling menu items (". . . sort of like barbecue, only with a different meat and a different sauce and, naturally, rice . . .") kept customers in stitches. Vinh did *his* share with quiet dignity that, he hoped, hid his discomfort with this new life.

Vinh looked over as another burst of laughter erupted at Song's table. She was at it again—"test-driving" a new menu idea.

"Really, they'd be great!" Song assured her chuckling audience. "Sort of a Vietnamese hush puppy . . . only not fried, and made with rice flour instead of cornmeal."

How does Song do that? Vinh wondered. *She somehow always seems to get what she expects.*

Come Asking

Like the boy I'd seen on the plane, Jesus, too, came away with something wonderful when he stood before his Father with an eager spirit and a willing heart. The day Jesus went to worship, his very face was changed!

You're telling me that Jesus went to worship?!

I am. The Bible speaks of a day when Jesus took time to stand with friends in the presence of God.

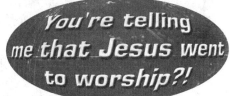

You're telling me that Jesus went to worship?!

A CHANGED FACE AND A SET OF WINGS

Six days later, Jesus took Peter, James, and John, the brother of James, up on a high mountain by themselves. While they watched, Jesus' appearance was changed; his face became bright like the sun, and his clothes became white as light. Then Moses and Elijah appeared to them, talking with Jesus.

Peter said to Jesus, "Lord, it is good that we are here. If you want, I will put up three tents here—one for you, one for Moses, and one for Elijah."

While Peter was talking, a bright cloud covered them. A voice came from the cloud and said, "This is my Son, whom I love, and I am very pleased with him. Listen to him!"

—MATTHEW 17:1–5 NCV

From Matthew's words, we know that Jesus made a *decision* to stand in the presence of God . . . and it was no spur-of-the-moment action. He didn't wake up one morning, look at the calendar and then at his watch, and say, "Oops, today is the day we go to the mountain." No, he had preparations to make.

Ministry to people was put on hold so ministry to his heart could occur. Since his chosen place of worship was some distance away, he had to select the right path and stay on the right road. By the time he was on the mountain, his heart was ready. Jesus prepared for worship.

Let me ask you, do you do the same? Do you prepare for worship? What paths do you take to lead you up the mountain? The question might seem a little strange, but my hunch is, many of us simply wake up and show up. We're sadly *casual* when it comes to meeting God.

Would we be so "unconcerned" with, oh, let's say, the president? Suppose you were granted a Sunday morning breakfast at the White House. How would you spend Saturday night? Would you get ready? Would you think about your questions and requests? Of course you would. Should we prepare any *less* for a meeting with the Holy God?

Let me urge you to come to worship *prepared* to worship. Pray before you come so you will be ready to pray when you arrive. Sleep before you come so you'll stay alert when you arrive. Read the Word before you come so your heart will be soft when you worship.

Come hungry. Come willing. Come expecting God to speak. Most of all, come asking, "Can I see the pilot today?"

> > > Frustrated as he was by his own awkwardness—and his sister's ease—at fitting in with American ways, Vinh did find much to admire in their adopted country.

Imagine . . . being able to say whatever you wanted to—right out loud—without getting in trouble with the authorities! (His father had said the wrong words to the wrong people once too often in their old land and was forced out of business.)

And so much of . . . everything! (A trip to the supermarket or the mall could still amaze the Tranhs with the abundance that everyone else seemed to take for granted.)

But so noisy, too . . . and everything moving so fast!

> > > > > > > > > > > >

"Doesn't it bother you, Song?" he'd asked once. "How impatient people are when you can't keep up?"

"Oh, I just do the best I can," she'd answered. "And most people are nice, if you expect them to be."

"You know, Song, not everybody wants to be your friend," he'd tried to warn her.

"Well, I know that," she'd answered. "I'm not stupid, Vinh—just hopeful! And how will I ever find out, if I just push everyone away first?" *Like you do,* she thought, but didn't say. *Oh, Vinh, if you'd only let them see what they're missing!*

And so it went. Song jumped into the "melting pot" that is America with a joyful splash; Vinh sometimes dipped in a cautious toe but never quite got past the feeling of being out of place, and . . . different.

"Well, goodness, Vinh," Song told him, "we are different! That's what America's all about. Everyone here— or at least an ancestor—is from somewhere else. And there's room for all of us . . . to be whoever we want to be. We don't have to stop being ourselves, you know; we just get to be ourselves in new and better ways!"

And that was a thought that brought Vinh face to face with a possibility he hadn't expected at all.

Reflecting His Glory

Come to worship expecting to meet God, and you'll discover the *purpose* of worship—to change the face of the worshiper. This is exactly what happened to Christ on the mountain. Jesus' appearance was changed: "His face became bright like the sun" (Matthew 17:2 NCV).

The connection between the face and worship isn't accidental, you know. Our face is the most public part of our bodies. It is also the most recognizable part of our bodies. We don't fill a school yearbook with photos of people's feet; we show faces.

God wants to take our faces, this most memorable part of us, and use them to reflect his goodness. Paul writes: "Our faces, then, are not covered. We all show the Lord's glory, and we are being changed to be like him. . . ." (2 Corinthians 3:18 NCV).

God invites us to see his face so he can change ours. He uses our uncovered faces to display his glory. The transformation isn't easy. The sculptor of Mount Rushmore faced a lesser challenge than does God. But our Lord is up to the task.

God loves to change the faces of his children. By his fingers, wrinkles of worry are rubbed away. Shadows of shame and doubt become portraits of grace and trust. His touch can turn tears of despair into tears of peace.

How? Through worship.

His touch can turn tears of despair into tears of peace.

We'd expect something more complicated, more demanding. Perhaps a forty-day fast or memorizing Leviticus. No. God's plan is simpler. He changes our faces through worship.

Exactly what *is* worship? I like King David's definition. "O magnify the LORD with me, and let us exalt His name together" (Psalm 34:3 NASB).

Worship is the act of *magnifying* God. *Enlarging* our vision of him. Stepping into the cockpit to see where he sits and how he works. Of course, his size doesn't change, but the way we see him does. As we draw nearer, he seems larger. And isn't that what we need? A *big* view of God? Don't we have *big* problems, *big* worries, *big* questions? Of course we do. That's why we need a big view of God.

Worship offers that. How can we sing "Holy, Holy, Holy" and not have our vision expanded . . . our faces brightened?

A vibrant, shining face is the mark of one who has stood in God's presence. After speaking with God, Moses had to cover his face with a veil (Exodus 34:33–35 NCV). After seeing heaven, Stephen's face glowed like that of an angel (Acts 6:15; 7:55–56 NCV).

God is in the business of changing the face of the world.

Let me be very clear. This change is his job, not ours. Our goal is not to make our faces shine. Not even Jesus did that. Matthew says, "Jesus' appearance was changed," not "Jesus changed his appearance." Our goal is not to come up with some fake, frozen expression. Our goal is simply to stand before God with a prepared and willing heart and then let God do his work.

And he does. He wipes away the tears. He smooths

away the worry. He touches our cheeks. He changes our faces as we worship.

But there's more. Not only does God change the face of those who worship, he changes those who *watch* us worship.

> › › › Vinh sighed as he watched his sister trans-form another table of strangers into her friends. Song moved so easily through this new world, while *he* seemed stuck in the past.
>
> It wasn't supposed to work that way! In their old life, it was Vinh, the wise big brother, who had always led the way, with his adoring little sister following in his footsteps.
>
> *But that was then, this is now. And who says wis-dom has an age . . . or a gender?!*
>
> › › › › › › › › › › › ›
>
> "It's really not that hard, Vinh," Song told him during their break after the dinner rush. "You just take the best of the old and the best of the new and mix them all together to make something . . . spectacular!"
>
> Vinh thought about that for a long moment, then he grinned. "Kind of like your Vietnamese hush puppies?"
>
> "Exactly." Song beamed.
>
> "You know, I'm not so sure those are going to catch on," he teased.
>
> "Well . . . they *might*. Especially if we *expect* them

to! But we'll *never* know unless we try. Kind of like with peop—"

Song stopped, worried about her brother's feelings. But he surprised her.

"Kind of like with people," he agreed. Then he frowned. "But I've been so busy pushing everyone away, that's all they'll expect from me now."

"Well . . . ," said Song with a grin, "you *could* surprise them! Besides, you know what Papa always says . . ."

Vinh nodded thoughtfully, then, with a smile, recited the Tranh family motto: "Anything is possible if you're willing to work hard enough!"

Evangelistic Worship

Remember the boy on the plane? His enthusiasm stirred me. I wanted to see the pilot, too.

The same thing happens when we come to worship with a heart of worship. Paul told the Corinthian church to worship in such a clear way that if an unbeliever entered, "he would find . . . the secrets of his heart revealed; and . . . would fall down on his face and worship God, declaring that God is indeed among you" (1 Corinthians 14:24–25 TJB).

Your heartfelt worship can be an inspiring example—as Jesus' worship was for Peter. Peter was so moved by what he saw in Jesus' face that he wanted to do something—*any-thing*—for God. So he offered to put up three tents to mark the holy place. He didn't understand that God wants hearts and not tents, but at least he was moved to give *something*.

Why? Because he saw the changed face of Christ. The same happens in churches today. When people see us giving heartfelt praise to God—when they hear our worship—they are curious. Sparks from *our* fire light *their* hearts. They want to see the pilot!

Seekers might not understand all that happens in a house of worship, but they know joy when they see it. And when they see *your* face changed, they might want to see God's face.

By the way, wouldn't the opposite be equally true? What happens when a seeker sees boredom in your face? Others are in his presence, but are you in your own little world? While others are seeking God's face, are you seeking the face of your wristwatch?

They are watching. Believe me. They are watching. And *you* have the chance to show them something wonderful. Just like Jesus did.

May I urge you to be just like Jesus? Prepare your heart for worship. Let God change your face through worship. Demonstrate the power of worship. Above all, seek the face of the pilot. The boy on the plane did. And because he did, he left with a changed face and a set of wings. The same can happen to you.

8 | GOLF GAMES AND CELERY STICKS

(A FOCUSED HEART)

I ask—ask the God of our Master,
Jesus Christ, the God of glory—to make
you intelligent and discerning in knowing
him personally, your eyes focused and
clear, so that you can see exactly what
it is he is calling you to do.
　　　　—EPHESIANS 1:17–18 MSG

The golf game was tied with four holes to go. I looked ahead to the next green. "Sure seems like a long way off," I said. No one spoke. "Sure is a narrow fairway," I said, placing my ball on the tee. Again, no response. "How do they expect us to hit over those trees?" Still no answer.

The silence didn't bother me. Years of ruthless golf competition against fellow ministers has taught me to be wary of their tricks. I knew exactly what they were doing: They were trying to psych me out (after all, we were playing for a soda). So I stepped up to the ball and took a swing. And—there's no other way to describe it—*I hit a great drive!*

As my ball soared over the crop of trees to my left, I could hear the other guys groan. I figured they were jealous. None of *them* even made it close to the trees. Rather than hit left as I had, they each hit to the right and ended up miles from the green. That's when I should have suspected something, but I didn't.

They walked down their side of the fairway, and I walked down mine. I finally found my ball, not on thick fairway grass, but buried in weeds and surrounded by trees.

"This sure is a tough hole," I muttered to myself. Never mind, I was up for the challenge. I studied the shot, took out a club, and—forgive me, but I must say it—*I hit another great shot.* The ball skimmed through the trees and headed toward the green like a jack rabbit dashing for supper. Only the steep hill kept it from rolling onto the putting surface.

From watching golf tournaments on TV, I knew exactly what to do next. I held my follow-through pose just long enough for the photographers to take their pictures, then I waved to the crowd. Of course, in my case there was no photographer or crowd. And my buddies were all on the other side of the fairway, looking in the other direction.

Again, it should have occurred to me that something was wrong. No one else commenting on the difficulty of the hole. No one complimenting my splendid drive. Everyone else hitting to the right while I hit to the left. It should have occurred to me, but it didn't.

Only as I neared the green did anything seem unusual. Some players were already putting—players I didn't know! I looked around for my group, and found them . . . on a *different* green.

That's when it hit me. I'd played the wrong hole! I had picked out the wrong target. All of a sudden everything made sense. My buddies hit to the right because they were supposed to. Their groan after my drive was one of pity, not envy. No wonder the hole seemed hard—I was playing in the wrong direction. How discouraging. Golf is tough enough as it is. It's even tougher when you're headed the wrong way.

The same can be said about life. Life is tough enough as it is. It's even tougher when we're headed in the wrong direction.

> > > The enthusiastic members of the Elm Street Church youth group had never met a good cause they *didn't* like. (Which, as it turned out, was both the good news *and* the bad news where they were concerned.) In fact, their schedule of activities was practically nonstop.

If they weren't washing cars to fund a mission project, they were painting a homeless shelter, or delivering meals to shut-ins, or volunteering at a day-care center, or involved in a dozen *other* ambitious projects. They were, in short . . . busy.

Maybe a little *too* busy? Kia loved being in the thick of things, and truly liked being helpful. And, truth be told, the *social* aspects of youth group activities were a *lot* of fun! Or at least they had been.

Lately, though, it seemed to Kia that things were a little . . . *off.* It was almost as if they were all missing the point somehow.

> . . . it seemed to Kia that things were a little . . . off.

The Heart on Target

One of the incredible abilities of Jesus was to stay on target. His life never got off track. Not once do we find him walking down the wrong side of the fairway. He had no money, no computers, no jets, no staff, yet Jesus did what many of us fail to do. He kept his life on course.

As Jesus looked across the horizon of his future, he could see many targets, each of which he could have pursued. He could have been a political revolutionary. He could have been a national leader. He could have been content to be a teacher and educate minds or be a physician and heal bodies. But in the end he chose to be a Savior and save souls.

Anyone near Christ for any length of time heard it from Jesus himself. "The Son of Man did not come to be served. He came to serve others and to give his life as a ransom for many people" (Mark 10:45 NCV).

The heart of Christ was faithfully focused on one task. The day he left the carpentry shop of Nazareth, he had one ultimate aim—the cross of Calvary. He was so focused that his final words were, "It is finished" (John 19:30 NCV).

How could Jesus say he was finished? There were still the hungry to feed, the sick to heal, the untaught to instruct, and the unloved to love. How could he say he was finished? Simple. He had completed his appointed task. His purpose was fulfilled. His job was done.

> › › › "It's like I can never get anything *finished!*" Kia sighed—slapping paint on the wall of the church nursery with more speed than accuracy. It was hard to concentrate on the mural with that not-nearly-done history paper on her mind. And who knew *when* she'd bake the cookies she'd promised for Saturday's bake sale!
>
> "Tell me about it!" chimed in Allie, who'd had quite a "discussion" with her mom just that afternoon about some undone household chores. But, really, how was she supposed to clean her room, finish her math, *and* organize a car wash with no—count 'em, *zero*—volunteers?!
>
> "At least *your* dad's not on your case about grades." That was Seth. "And why are we out of blue *and* green paint?" he grumbled. "Who's in charge of supplies anyway? Oh," he said, as several pointed glances—and a glare or two—reminded him that *he* was.

It wasn't just Kia, you see, who was starting to notice a few bumps in the road. Everyone in the usually smooth-running youth group seemed to be feeling the effects. Tempers were shorter. Griping was up and cooperation way down. Even worse, nothing they did seemed to be *fun* anymore.

"Uh, Kia?" That was Allie, eyeing the half-finished wall. "Did you really mean to paint *three* lambs? I thought two of anything was the limit on Noah's Ark."

"Oh, no!" Normally, Kia would have laughed it off with a quip about unexpected triplets. But the jokes, too, had been few and far between lately. "What's *wrong* with me? I just can't seem to keep things *together* anymore!"

Distracted Hearts

Our lives tend to be so scattered—with no strategy, no goal, no clear purpose. Playing the holes out of order. Living life with the hiccups! So distracted by the small things that we forget the big things—like the celery lady did. Saturday. In my favorite section of the grocery store—the sample section.

As always, I headed straight for the back of the store where the samplers tend to linger. Bingo! There were two of them. One had a skillet of sausage and the other a plate of cream-cheese-stuffed celery. You'll be proud to know I chose the celery. I wanted the sausage, but I knew the celery was better for me.

Unfortunately, the celery lady never saw me. She was too

busy straightening her celery sticks. I walked past her, and she never looked up. The sausage lady, however, saw me coming and held out the plate. I said, "No thanks," and made another circle past the celery lady. She still didn't see me. She was too busy tidying up her plate. So I made another loop past the sausage lady. Once again the offer came, and once again I resisted. I was committed to doing the right thing.

So was the celery lady. She was determined to get every celery stick in perfect order. I stopped. I coughed. I cleared my throat. I did everything but sing a song. Still no response. The sausage lady, however, was still waiting. I gave in; I ate the sausage.

The celery lady made the same mistake I had made on the golf course. She got off target. She was so busy with the small matters (celery organization) that she forgot her assignment (to help needy, hungry, pitiful shoppers like me).

How do we keep from making the same mistake in life? God wants us to be just like Jesus and have focused hearts. How do I choose the right direction and stay on target? Checking the map would be a good start. I would have saved myself a lot of hassle that day on the golf course had I taken time to look at the map on the scorecard. The golf course architect had drawn one. What's true on the golf course is true

How do I choose the right direction and stay on target?

in life as well. The one who designed *our* course left us directions. Of course, we *do* have to check the "map" from time to time—*and* pay attention.

> > > "C'mon, guys, pay attention . . . *PLEASE!*" But nobody took the slightest notice of Jason's frustrated plea. In spite of their new student ministry intern's best efforts, the meeting had just dissolved into total chaos. It all started during a discussion of the plans for Vacation Bible School. The games, skits, and crafts their group did each year to teach and entertain the younger kids were now legendary. The pressure was intense—they had a reputation to uphold!

Karen set things off with a question—and a side glance at Amy—about why "*some* people seem to get all the neat jobs, while the rest of us do the dirty work."

"Because," Amy flashed back, "*some* people can be counted on to show up when they say they will!"

"Speaking of showing up"—that was Allie, seizing her moment—"not one of you has even *signed* up for the car wash. I can't do it alone, you know!"

"Why not?" snapped Drew. "That's what Kia and I had to do at the Senior Center last week!"

And they were off and running. Everyone had some kind of complaint or criticism or frustration to air as loudly as possible. Jason was shocked and embarrassed. Clearly, his "advising" skills needed work. And this meeting needed *order!* His piercing whistle filled the room. In the sudden silence that followed, every-one was very busy looking at the floor, the ceiling, their shoes—*anywhere*, in fact, but at each other.

"Wow," said Jason, then, "Guys, I think we have a problem."

"I wondered when someone was going to notice," said a quiet voice from the back of the room.

Every head whipped around to stare at Minister Hal Winters, who rarely spoke up at their meetings. Their minister was a "low-profile" kind of adviser—operating with an amused eye on their antics and a light hand on the reins.

"Feeling a little stressed-out, are we? Maybe a little out of . . . focus?" he asked with a grin.

Their silent nods signaled the *first* agree-ment of the evening.

"Feeling a little stressed-out, are we?"

It was Kia, finally, who spoke up: "What I don't understand is why doing good should make us feel so . . . *bad!*"

"Shouldn't," said Mr. Winters, "unless . . . you're maybe doing a little too *much* good?"

What?!

"But how can that be?" asked Jason. "What can possibly be *wrong* with doing the *right* thing?!"

"Unless . . . ," repeated the minister, who was more likely to toss out clues than answers, "unless you're doing the right thing for the *wrong* reasons."

Smiling at their blank looks, he gave them one more little . . . nudge. "Anybody done a reality check lately on *why* you're doing what you're doing?"

Well, of course, we know why! We're doing it because . . . because . . .

Which led to exactly the kind of soul-searching—and map-checking—that the minister had in mind all along.

Checking the map isn't all that difficult, you know. With just four simple questions we can be more like Jesus; we can stay on course with our lives.

1. Am I fitting into God's plan? Romans 8:28 says, "We know that all that happens to us is working for our good if we love God and are fitting into his plans" (TLB). The first step in focusing your heart is to ask this question: Am I fitting into God's plan?

God's plan is to save his children. And if God's goal is the salvation of the world, then our goal should be the same. "We're Christ's representatives. God uses us to persuade men and women" (2 Corinthians 5:20 MSG). You are intended to contribute to the good plan of God, to tell others about the God who loves them and longs to bring them home.

But exactly *how* are you to do that? What is *your* specific assignment? Let's seek the answer with another question.

2. What are my longings? Surprised? Maybe you thought your longings had nothing to do with keeping your life on track. Wrong! Your heart is very important. Psalm 37:4 says, "Enjoy serving the LORD, and he will give you what you want" (NCV). When we submit to God's plans, we can trust our desires. Our assignment is found at the meeting place of God's plan and our pleasures. *What do you love to do? What brings you joy? What gets you excited?*

Each of us has been made to serve God in a special way. "We are God's workmanship, created in Christ Jesus to do good works, which God prepared in advance for us to do" (Ephesians 2:10 NIV).

You are a custom design. God planned you before you were born. You are not an accident. The longings of your heart, then, are not accidental; they are important messages. The desires of your heart are to be listened to. God is too gracious to ask you to do something you hate.

Be careful, though. Don't consider your desires without considering your skills.

3. What are my abilities? There are some things we *want* to do but simply aren't equipped for. I, for example, would love to sing. Unfortunately, I can't carry a tune in a bucket!

Paul gives good advice in Romans 12:3: "Have a sane estimate of your capabilities" (PHILLIPS).

In other words, know your strengths. When you teach, do people listen? When you lead, do people follow? When you take charge, do things improve? Identify your strengths, then—this is important—major in them. Take a few irons out of the fire so the *best* ones can get hot.

We cannot meet every need in the world. We cannot

satisfy every request in the world. Have a sane estimate of your abilities and stick to them. And be sure to ask the final question.

4. Am I serving God now? That's a pretty heavy question, and it might start you wondering . . . *Maybe I should give up soccer or piano. Do I really want to be a teacher or marine biologist? Maybe Max is telling me I need to go to seminary. . . .* Hold it! Don't get carried away with making—or changing—plans for your life. Jesus gave us a *better* example of fulfilling our purpose.

When do we get our first clue that Jesus knows he is the Son of God? In the Temple of Jerusalem. He is twelve years old. His parents are three days into the return trip to Nazareth before they notice he is missing. They find him in the Temple studying with the leaders. When his parents ask him for an explanation, he says, "Did you not know that I must be about My Father's business?" (Luke 2:49 NKJV).

As a young boy, Jesus already senses the call of God. But what does he do next? Recruit apostles and preach sermons and perform miracles? No, he goes home to his folks and learns the family business.

Want to bring focus to your life? Do what Jesus did. Go home, love your family, and "take care of business."

But Max, I'm ready to do great things for God. Good, do them at school. Be a good student. Show up on time with a good attitude. Don't complain or grumble, but "work as if you were doing it for the Lord, not for people" (Colossians 3:23 NCV).

> > > It's amazing what a little soul-searching, and a lot of honesty, can accomplish—as the youth group discovered. They knew they were in trouble. So they threw themselves—no holds barred, as usual—into figuring out *why*.

They weren't very proud of some of the answers—and definitely *embarrassed* when they took a hard look at some of their recent projects: the car washes where the focus was more on goofing off than cleaning cars. The rushed-through visits at the Senior Center, so there'd be time for pizza afterward. The projects reluctantly taken on, and halfheartedly done, because they had a "reputation" to uphold. And *all* the other things in their lives they'd neglected in order to do more and more, with less and less *care*.

"Oh, my," said Kia, "we're *way* off course. We started out serving God, and ended up serving ourselves! *What* were we thinking?!"

"You weren't," said Jason. "You were just running as fast as you could . . . in the *wrong* direction—and I wasn't in the lead, where I should have been."

"So," asked the ever-practical Karen, "what's our plan for getting *back* on track?"

And that set them all off again. Only *this* time they were working together . . . and knew where they were going . . . and *why*.

And, oh, yes, the fun came back, too.

The P.L.A.N.

There's an excellent plan for keeping *your* life on track. All you have to do is keep four key letters in mind—and ask the right questions:

Am I fitting into God's **P**lan?
What are my **L**ongings?
What are my **A**bilities?
Am I serving God **N**ow?

Why don't you take a few moments and check your direction? Ask yourself the four questions. You might find that you are doing what I did: hitting some good shots but in the wrong direction.

But here's the good news! God allows you to start fresh at any point in life. "From now on, then, you must live the rest of your earthly lives controlled by God's will and not by human desires" (1 Peter 4:2 TEV).

Circle the words *from now on*. God will give you a fresh scorecard. Regardless of where you were headed before, it's never too late—or too early—to get your life on course and be a part of God's P.L.A.N.

> *God allows you to start fresh at any point in life.*

9 NOTHING BUT THE TRUTH

(AN HONEST HEART)

So from now on,
there must be no more
lies. Speak the truth
to one another.
—EPHESIANS 4:25 TJB

A woman stands before judge and jury, places one hand on the Bible and the other in the air, and makes a pledge. For the next few minutes, with God as her helper, she will "tell the truth, the whole truth, and nothing but the truth."

She is a witness. Her job is not to add to nor take away from the truth. Her job is to tell the truth. Leave it to the lawyers to interpret. Leave it to the jury to decide. Leave it to the judge to apply. But the witness? The witness speaks the truth. Let her do more or less and she taints the outcome.

But let her do that—let her tell the truth—and justice has a chance.

The Christian, too, is a witness. We, too, make a pledge. Like the witness in court, we are called to tell the truth. The bench might be absent and the judge unseen, but the Bible is present, the watching world is the jury, and *we* are the primary witnesses. We are called to serve by no less than Jesus himself: "You will be my *witnesses*—in Jerusalem, in all of Judea, in Samaria, and in every part of the world" (Acts 1:8 NCV, italics mine).

We are witnesses. And like witnesses in a court, we are called to testify, to tell what we have seen and heard. And we are to speak truthfully. Our job is not to whitewash nor puff up the truth. Our task is to tell the truth. Period.

Our task is to tell the truth. Period.

There is, however, one difference between the witness in court and the witness for Christ. The witness in court sooner or later steps down from the witness chair, but the witness for Christ never does. Since the claims of Christ are always on trial, court is always in session, and we remain under oath. For the Christian, deception is never an option. It wasn't an option for Jesus.

> ❯ ❯ ❯ It wasn't a possibility everyone would get excited about, but, for Jeff, it would be the absolute *coolest* summer job ever! Well, not exactly "job"—all

those long hours in the hot sun would be strictly vol-
unteer. And he couldn't wait to get started. Of course,
first, he had to actually land the job.

Jeff—and his best buddy, Luke—had been waiting for
years for their shot as counselors at Pleasant Hills
Christian Day Camp. Ever since they first went to day
camp as little guys, they'd both had their sights set on
those envied, admired jobs. At last, as eighth graders,
they were finally eligible to be junior counselors. And
wouldn't you know . . . *this* year the rules changed!
Instead of counselors being chosen from a citywide pool
of applicants, there would now be just *one* junior and
one senior counselor from *each* participating church.

Suddenly, the two best friends were "best rivals" for
the job they'd always expected to be doing *together*.
And that presented some unexpected problems—not the
least of which was honesty.

What God Can't Do

One of the most astounding statements about Christ is in
this summary: "He had done nothing wrong, and he had
never lied" (Isaiah 53:9 NCV). Jesus was always honest. His
every word accurate, his every sentence true.

No cheating on tests. No altering the
accounts. Not once did Jesus stretch
the truth. Not once did he shade the
truth. Not once did he avoid the
truth. He simply told the truth.

Jesus was always honest.

And if God has his way with us, we will do the same. He longs for us to be just like Jesus. He seeks not to have us lie *less* but to have us lie *not at all*. Never. Not for any reason. God is blunt about dishonesty: "No one who is dishonest will live in my house" (Psalm 101:7 NCV).

Our Master has a strict honor code. From Genesis to Revelation, the theme is the same: God loves the truth and hates deceit. In 1 Corinthians 6:9–10, Paul lists the type of people who will not inherit the kingdom of God. The group he portrays is a ragged assortment of those who worship idols, sell their bodies, get drunk, rob people, and—there it is—*lie about others.*

Such strictness might surprise you. *You mean my fibbing and flattering stir the same heavenly anger as aggravated assault?* Seems like it. God views fudging on the truth the same way he views kneeling before idols.

> The LORD hates those who tell lies but is pleased with those who keep their promises.
>
> —PROVERBS 12:22 NCV

Why? Why the hard line? Why the tough standard?

For one reason: Dishonesty is absolutely contrary to the character of God. According to Hebrews 6:18, *it is impossible for God to lie.* It's not that God will not lie or that he has chosen not to lie—*he cannot lie.* For God to lie is for a dog to fly and a bird to bark. It simply cannot happen.

God always speaks the truth. When he makes an agreement, he keeps it. When he makes a statement, he means it. And when he proclaims the truth, we can believe it. What he says is true.

Satan, on the other hand, finds it impossible to tell the truth. Jesus called him "the father of lies" (John 8:44 NCV). If you'll remember, deceit was the first tool out of the devil's bag. In the Garden of Eden, Satan didn't lure Eve or sneak up on her. He just lied to her. "God says you'll die if you eat the fruit? You will not die" (see Genesis 3:1–4 NCV).

BIG FAT LIAR! But Eve was suckered, and the fruit was plucked, and the damage was done. We've been playing games with the truth ever since. And we know better!

〉 〉 〉 Nobody knew better than Jeff and Luke what it took to make a great camp counselor. After all, they'd spent years working toward that goal.

There wasn't a camp game or activity or skill they hadn't mastered. From the lakeshore to the top of the climbing tower, from horseback to backpack, from beadwork to Bible study, if one of them wasn't leading the way, the other was. And nobody had more talent for having—and *creating*—fun than those two "live wires."

The truth was, finding two better choices for camp counselor would be hard to do. But not *nearly* as hard as the choice Jeff was faced with Wednesday evening!

It was a simple announcement that was read aloud at the youth group meeting, then posted on the bulletin board as a reminder. Most of the kids didn't pay it much attention. Jeff, on the other hand, didn't hear anything else. The deadline for counselor applications had been moved up to this Friday! Instead of two weeks, there were now just two *days*—and Luke wasn't there to get the news!

The rest of the meeting went right over Jeff's head. He was busy with a problem of . . . ethics. Should he tell Luke about the deadline change? *After all, he is my best friend.* Why *should* he tell Luke? *After all, it was his choice to skip tonight's meeting!*

'Round and 'round the questions went: What was fair? What was right? What was smart? *After all, he is my biggest competition. And I really want this job!* But so, he knew, did Luke.

Then Minister Carter complicated things even more—by handing him an extra copy of the notice. "I know Luke is really interested in this. Could you make sure he knows about the new deadline?"

He is my biggest competition. And I really want this job!

Yikes! "Uh . . . sure. I guess. No problem." But it *was* a problem—a big one. Because now, instead of only a question of ethics, he was also face-to-face with the "honesty" thing, too. And *that*, as his parents had made sure he well knew, was a very big deal, indeed!

"Truth, Jeff," they'd always insisted, "is nonnegotiable. It's okay to have a great imagination. It's okay to add a little 'color' to make a story more interesting. But it's *never* okay to *change* the truth!"

And, of course, they were right. No question about that. But still . . . *Why me? Why now?!*

Maybe the question shouldn't be "Why does God demand such honesty?" but rather "Why do *we* put up with such dishonesty?" Never was Jeremiah more the prophet than when he announced: "The heart is deceitful above all things". (Jeremiah 17:9 NIV). How do we explain our dishonesty? What's the reason for our forked tongues and slippery promises?

For one thing, we don't like the truth. Most of us can sympathize with the fellow who received a call from his wife just as she was about to fly home from Europe. "How's my cat?" she asked.

"Dead."

"Oh, honey, don't be so honest. Why didn't you break the news to me slowly? You've ruined my trip."

"What do you mean?"

"You could have told me he was on the roof. And when I called you again from Paris, you could have told me he was acting tired. Then when I called from London, you could have said he was sick, and when I called you from New York, you could have said he was at the vet. Then when I got home, you could have said he was dead."

Such a plan had never occurred to the husband, but he was willing to learn. "Okay," he said. "I'll do better next time."

"By the way," she asked, "how's Mom?"

There was a long silence, then he replied, "Uh, she's on the roof."

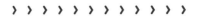

The plain fact is, we don't like the truth. Our motto is, *You shall know the truth, and the truth shall make you squirm.* Our dislike for the truth began at the age of three when

Mom walked into our room and asked, "Did you hit your little brother?" We knew then and there that honesty had its consequences. So we learned to, uhhh, well, it's not *really* lying . . . we learned to cover things up.

"Did I hit my baby brother? That all depends on what you mean by the word *hit*. I mean, sure I made contact with him, but would a jury consider it a 'hit'? Everything is relative, you know."

"Did I hit my baby brother? Yes, Dad, I did. But it's not my fault. Had I been born with nonaggressive genes and had you not let me watch television, it would never have happened. So, you can say I hit my brother, but the fault isn't mine. I'm a victim here, too."

The truth, we learn early, is not fun. We don't like the truth.

Not only do we not like the truth, *we don't trust the truth.* If we are brutally honest (which is a good idea in a discussion about honesty), we'd have to admit there are times when the truth doesn't get the job done that we *need* done.

We want our teachers or coaches to like us, so we flatter. We call it polishing the apple. God calls it a lie.

We want people to admire us, so we exaggerate. We call it stretching the truth. God calls it a lie.

We want people to respect us, so we buy things we can't afford and charge bills we can't pay. We call it the American way. God calls it living a lie.

> ❯ ❯ ❯ There are times when truth can be a not-so-comfortable bedfellow, as Jeff found out that sleepless Wednesday night. His brain just wouldn't "turn off."

Instead, it kept twisting and turning through elaborate schemes that would allow him to do the impossible: keep his word to Minister Carter, *without* giving up the advantage of knowing something Luke didn't. And, of course, there was also the issue of doing right by his friend.

The later it got, the more inventive became Jeff's rationalizations:

Okay, I said I'd give him the notice . . . but I didn't say when, *did I?* (As if getting the word about the deadline too late would do Luke any good!)

What if I just don't happen to run into him at school tomorrow? (As if Jeff and Luke didn't gravitate together like two magnets between *every* class!)

Finally, in desperation . . . *What if I somehow lost the notice? Hey, accidents happen!* (As if the date weren't engraved in Jeff's brain . . . and he didn't have a voice.)

Even that old standby, too-sick-to-go-to-school, didn't cut it. His temperature was disgustingly *normal* the next morning—and he was no closer to a solution!

And, of course, running under all Jeff's inventive plots to *avoid* telling the truth without actually *lying,* were two *other* truths: Honesty *is* nonnegotiable, and Luke deserved this chance just as much as Jeff did. And, wiggle as he would, that *was* the truth.

If We Don't Tell the Truth

Ananias and Sapphira represent just how much we humans do not trust the truth. They sold a piece of property and gave half of the money to the church. They lied to Peter and the apostles, claiming that the land sold for the amount they gave. Their sin was not in keeping some of the money for themselves; it was in twisting the truth. Their deceit resulted in their deaths. Luke writes: "The whole church and all the others who heard about these things were filled with fear" (Acts 5:11 NCV).

More than once I've heard people refer to this story with a nervous chuckle and say, "I'm glad God doesn't still strike people dead for lying." I'm not so sure he doesn't. It seems to me that the wages of deceit is still death. Not death of the body, perhaps, but the death of:

▸▸ *a friendship*—Falsehoods are termites in the trunk of the relationship tree.

▸▸ *a conscience*—The tragedy of the second lie is that it is always easier to tell than the first.

▸▸ *a goal*—Just ask the student who got booted out for cheating, if the lie wasn't fatal.

▸▸ *faith*—The language of faith and the language of falsehood have two different vocabularies. Those who are experts in the language of falsehood find terms like *confession* and *repentance* hard to pronounce.

We could also list the deaths of intimacy, trust, peace, credibility, and self-respect. But perhaps the most tragic death that occurs from deceit is our witness. The court won't listen to the testimony of a lying witness. Neither will the world. Do we think people will believe our words about Christ when they can't believe our words about other things? Even more important, do we think God will use us as a witness if we won't tell the truth?

Every high school football team has a player whose assignment is to carry the play from the coach to the huddle. What if the player doesn't tell the truth? What if the coach calls for a pass but the messenger says the coach called for a run? One thing is certain: The coach won't call on that player very long. God says if we are faithful with the small things, he'll trust us with the greater things (Matthew 25:21 NCV). Can he trust you with the small things?

〉 〉 〉 Give Jeff credit for one thing—and not a small one at that: Through all his mental acrobatics, he never once tried to tell himself that *he* would be a better camp counselor than Luke. The truth was, they'd *both* be great.

True, Jeff did know every camp song ever written— and some he'd made up on the spot. And nobody could tell a ghost story like he could! He was also neck and neck with Luke when it came to sports and games and camp skills. Ah, but Luke was a much better teacher and encourager and *sharer* of skills—which, after all, was what counselors *did*.

And there was one other inescapable issue—the whole point of Christian camp: helping kids grow into the kind of people God wants them to be. *And that means building—and demonstrating—character . . . especially in counselors!*

Faith, Truth, Values . . . Character. He'd be turning his back on all those things if he was less than honest with Luke now! Which, by the time he reached school Thursday morning, made the "tough" decision a real no-brainer.

> > > > > > > > > > > >

"Hey, Luke," Jeff called, catching up with his buddy, "got something for you—something I almost didn't give you; if you want to know the truth."

Luke barely glanced at the notice. "Nah," he said, "I knew you'd do the right thing."

"You knew?! About the deadline?"

"Sure," said Luke. "Minister Carter called last night, just in case we missed connections. 'No problem,' I told him. 'Jeff will come through, like always.'"

Then, with a grin at the look on Jeff's face, Luke went on, "Of course, I *didn't* mention you might have to think it over first."

Facing the Music

The cure for deceit is simply this: Face the music. Tell the truth. Some of us are living in deceit. Some of us are walking in the shadows. The lies of Ananias and Sapphira resulted in death; so have ours. Some of us have buried a friendship, parts of a conscience, and even parts of our faith—all because we won't tell the truth.

What *should* you do when you're wondering if you should tell the truth or not? The question to ask in such moments is, Will God bless my deceit? Will he who hates lies bless a strategy built on lies? Will the Lord, who loves the truth, bless the business of falsehoods? Will God honor the career of the liar? Will God come to the aid of the cheater? Will God bless my dishonesty?

I don't think so, either.

Examine your heart. Ask yourself some tough questions.

Am I being completely honest with my parents and teachers and friends? Are my relationships marked by truth? Am I honest in my dealings? Am I a trustworthy student? An honest friend? A reliable witness?

Do you tell the truth . . . always?

If not, start today. Don't wait until tomorrow. The ripple of today's lie is tomorrow's wave and next year's flood. Start today. Be just like Jesus. Tell the truth, the whole truth, and nothing but the truth.

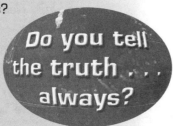

Do you tell the truth . . . always?

10 THE GREENHOUSE OF THE MIND

(A PURE HEART)

Be self-controlled and alert. Your enemy the devil prowls around like a roaring lion looking for someone to devour. Resist him, standing firm in the faith.
—1 PETER 5:8–9 NIV

› › › *Had* there been a school election—two years ago—to choose a "Miss Negativity," Julie Fairchild would have won hands-down.

To look at her, it was hard to imagine that a girl as delicate and pretty as a flower would have such a *thorny* attitude. But Julie could see the rain in every cloud, a tornado in every breeze—and the put-down in every friendly smile.

No question about it, Julie lived in a very *weedy* "garden"—one that definitely needed some serious digging and pruning.

Suppose you come to visit me one day and find me working in my greenhouse. (Neither my house nor my thumb is green, but let's pretend.) I explain to you that the greenhouse was a gift from my father. He used state-of-the-art equipment to create the ideal place for growth. The air is perfect. The lighting exact. The temperature is suited for flowers, fruit, or anything I want, and what I want is flowers and fruit.

I ask you to join me as I collect some seeds to plant. You've always thought I was a bit crazy, but what I do next removes all doubt. You watch me walk into a field and strip seeds off weeds. I fill a bag with a variety of weed seeds and return to the greenhouse.

You can't believe what you've just seen. "I thought you wanted a greenhouse full of flowers and fruit."

"I do."

"Then don't you think you ought to plant flower seeds and fruit seeds?"

"Do you have any idea how much those seeds cost? Besides, you have to drive all the way to the garden center to get them. No thanks, I'm taking the cheap and easy way."

You walk away mumbling something about one brick short of a load.

The Greenhouse of the Heart

All actions have consequences. Everybody knows you harvest what you sow. You reap what you plant. Yet strangely, what we know when it comes to gardening, we tend to forget when it comes to our hearts.

Think for a moment of your heart as a greenhouse. It, too, is a magnificent gift from your Father. It, too, is perfectly suited for growing. And your heart, like a greenhouse, has to be managed.

Consider for a moment your thoughts as seed. Some thoughts become flowers. Others become weeds. Sow seeds of hope and enjoy a positive outlook. Sow seeds of doubt and expect insecurity. "People harvest only what they plant" (Galatians 6:7 NCV).

The proof is everywhere you look. Ever wonder why some people seem to be able to resist negative thinking and remain patient, upbeat, and forgiving? Could it be that they have carefully sown seeds of goodness and are enjoying the harvest?

> Some thoughts become flowers. Others become weeds.

Ever wonder why others have such a sour outlook? Such a gloomy attitude? You would, too, if your heart were a greenhouse of weeds and thorns.

We reap the harvest of our weedy thoughts. Let's pause and think about that. If the heart is a greenhouse and our thoughts are seeds, shouldn't we be careful about what we sow? Shouldn't we be selective about the seeds we allow to come into the greenhouse? Shouldn't there be a guard at the door? Isn't guarding our heart and thoughts an important task? According to the Bible, it is. "Be careful what you think, because your thoughts run your life" (Proverbs 4:23 NCV).

> > >   Snap judgments about people and situations were Julie's specialty: "She's so stuck-up" . . . "He thinks he's so smart" . . . "Oh, I could never do *that!*" Which made for a pretty negative little world, a lot of missed opportunities, and an attitude that invited people to make those same sorts of judgments about *her.*

Spend much time with Julie, and even the most determined optimist could come down with a case of "gloom and doom." Which, naturally, meant people didn't spend much time with Julie. And that, naturally, just confirmed her worst suspicions!

Her parents had tried *everything* to get her to lighten up and look on the bright side. "Life is full of good things, sweetheart . . . if you look for them," was the parental theme. But Julie was always so busy anticipating the next disaster that she never saw any-thing else.

Did she *like* being that way? Not much. By sixth grade, even *she* was horrified at some of the things that popped out of her mouth. But by then, the rut she was stuck in was pretty deep—and she couldn't see *any* way out. Until the class play. And Miss Rutledge.

Fresh out of college and overflowing with enthusiasm, Anna Rutledge was every kid's dream teacher. Her off-the-wall sense of humor kept them all in stitches. And her talent for challenging—and *trusting*—her students won every heart. So when Miss Rutledge decided they were going to have a class play—a musical!—everyone, naturally, wanted to be in it. Even Julie. Especially Julie.

What was I thinking? There's no way I'll get a part, even though I am a better singer than most of—Oh, no, I'm doing it again!

With a sigh, Julie turned away from the audition sign-up sheet. Then she turned back, and took out a pen. Then she put the pen back in her bag, and turned away again.

"Having trouble deciding which part you want, Julie?"

Julie jumped. Miss Rutledge had somehow . . . *materialized* . . . right beside her!

"Oh, you know . . . ," Julie mumbled, "I'm probably not what you're looking for."

Miss Rutledge *did* know. She made it a point to know about all her students—especially the ones who needed a little help. "Why not?" she asked. "You've got a great singing voice *and*, I've heard, quite a talent for . . . 'drama.'"

What?! Julie knew that

> *Julie mumbled, "I'm probably not what you're looking for."*

a lot of kids called her "the drama queen." *Is she making fun of me?* But Miss Rutledge's smile was warm and friendly—though there *was* a glint of humor dancing in her eyes.

"Actually, Julie, I think your talent for convincing yourself of just about anything is *exactly* what this play needs! Though we might want to try a slightly *different* spin on some things," said Miss Rutledge, holding out a pen. "What do you say? We'll take a chance on you, if you'll take a chance on us."

This is probably a terrible idea! But it was practically impossible to refuse Miss Rutledge anything. So Julie took the pen. And signed up, though she didn't know it then, for a lot more than just the play.

Let's look at this thoughts-run-your-life idea from another angle. Suppose I ask you to take care of my house while I'm out of town. You pledge to keep everything in great shape. But when I return, I find the place is a mess. The carpet is torn, walls are smeared, furniture is broken. Your explanation is not impressive: Some bikers came by and needed a place to stay. Then the football team called, looking for a place to party. Then there were those three *very* wet, stray dogs that looked so *pitiful* out there in the rain. . . .

As the owner, I have one question: "Don't you know how to say no? This is not your house. You don't have the right to let in everyone and everything that wants to enter."

Ever think God wants to say the same to us?

Guarding Our Hearts

You've got to admit some of our hearts are trashed out. Let any riffraff knock on the door, and we throw it open. Anger shows up, and we let him in. Revenge needs a place to stay, so we have him pull up a chair. Pity wants to have a party, so we show him the kitchen. Don't we know how to say no?

Many don't. For most of us, thought management is, well, unthought of. We think a lot about time management, weight management, even scalp management. But what about thought management? Shouldn't we be as concerned about managing our thoughts as we are about managing anything else? Jesus was. Like a trained soldier at the gate of a city, he stood watch over his mind. He stubbornly guarded the gateway of his heart. Many thoughts were denied entrance. Need a few examples?

How about arrogance? On one occasion the people were determined to make Jesus their king. Most of us would delight in the notion of royalty. Not Jesus. "Jesus saw that in their enthusiasm, they were about to grab him and make him king, so he slipped off and went back up the mountain to be by himself" (John 6:15 MSG).

Or what about Peter when Jesus announced his coming death on the cross? "Impossible, Master! That can never be!" (Matthew 16:22 MSG). Apparently, Peter was about to question the necessity of Calvary. But he never had a chance. Christ blocked the doorway. "Peter, get out of my way. Satan, get lost. You have no idea how God works" (Matthew 16:23 MSG).

Have you ever had people laugh at you? Jesus did, too. When asked to heal a sick girl, he entered her house only to be told she was dead. His response? "The child is not dead but sleeping." The response of the people in the house? "They laughed at him." Just like all of us, Jesus had to face a moment of humiliation. But unlike most of us, he refused to receive it. "He put them all outside" (Mark 5:39–40 RSV).

Jesus guarded his heart. If he did, shouldn't we do the same? Most certainly! Jesus wants your heart to be fertile and fruitful. He wants you to have a heart like his. But how? The answer is surprisingly simple. We can be transformed if we make one decision: *I will submit my thoughts to the authority of Jesus.*

Jesus has the ultimate say on everything, especially our thoughts. "All authority in heaven and on earth has been given to me" (Matthew 28:18 NIV). There might be times, for instance, when you tell yourself you are worthless or a loser or too bad to be forgiven, but Jesus has a different opinion. If you give him authority over you, then your put-down thoughts are no longer allowed.

Jesus also has authority over your ideas. Suppose you have an idea that you want to rob a grocery store. Jesus, however, has made it clear that stealing is wrong. If you have given him authority over your ideas, then the idea of stealing cannot remain in your thoughts.

See what I mean by authority? To have a pure heart, we must submit all thoughts to the authority of Christ. If we are willing to do that, he will change us to be like him.

> > > "It all starts in your *minds,* people . . . in your minds!" It was Miss Rutledge's favorite speech. If she said it once, she said it hundreds of times during the weeks of rehearsal. "What you show your audience on the outside is what you create first. . . . Where, Andrew? . . . Where, Beth? . . . Where, Julie?"

"On the inside!" they'd obediently answer—then crack up at Miss Rutledge's exuberant, "*Yes,* my talented little geniuses!"

There was a lot of cracking up at those rehearsals—as much fun as there was hard work. And they *did* work hard. Miss Rutledge expected it. And *they'd* made up their minds that *this* play was going to be terrific. It was. And so were they. Especially—to her amazement, and everyone else's—Julie.

There had been a lot of eye-rolling when Julie was cast in one of the leading roles. The girl with the negative attitude playing upbeat, fun-loving Maria?! *How is* that *ever going to* work?!

"Think positive," was Anna Rutledge's response

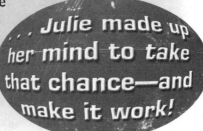

. . . Julie made up her mind to take that chance—and make it work!

to the head-shakers and naysayers. "Think positive," was her advice to Julie, too. And, because she knew she had been given a chance she hadn't done anything to deserve, Julie made up her mind to *take* that chance—and make it work!

Was it easy? No, especially in the first weeks, when Julie was *positive* everyone expected her to mess up. (Not exactly the kind of "positive" thinking Miss Rutledge had in mind.) Did she stumble and fall more than a few times on this new road? You bet. (Shuffling your entire way of thinking into a new—positive—mind-set doesn't happen overnight.) Did she quit? *Positive*-ly not!

Julie discovered she actually *liked* her funny, friendly, optimistic Maria character. And the deeper she dug to find "Maria" inside Julie, the less time she had to be critical about *other* people—who, it turned out, were a lot nicer and friendlier than she'd ever dreamed.

By opening night, she had the part nailed. In fact, she liked Maria's attitude so much, she really hated to give it up when the curtain came down. Then—at the cast party, where she felt right at home—it struck her: *Who says I have to?!*

Did Julie *become* Maria? No. Even better, she worked on becoming the best *Julie* she could be. Of course, she *did* have to keep a close eye on things . . . just to be sure none of those old familiar negative thoughts tried to sneak back "home."

The Guard at the Doorway

Your heart is a fertile greenhouse ready to produce good fruit. Your mind is the doorway to your heart—the place where you decide which seeds are sown and which seeds are discarded. The Holy Spirit is ready to help you manage and filter the thoughts that try to enter. He can help you guard your heart.

He stands with you on the threshold. A thought approaches, a questionable thought. Do you throw open the door and let it enter? Of course not. You "fight to capture every thought until it acknowledges the authority of Christ" (2 Corinthians 10:5 PHILLIPS). You don't leave the door unguarded. You stand equipped with handcuffs and leg irons, ready to capture any thought not fit to enter.

Let's say a thought regarding your personal value approaches. Like a neighborhood bully, the thought swaggers up to the door and says, "You're a loser. All your life, you've been a loser. You might as well write the word *bum* on your backpack, for that is what you are."

The ordinary person would throw open the door and let the thought in. Like a seed from a weed, it would find fertile soil and take root and bear thorns of inferiority. The average person would say, "You're right. I'm a bum. Come on in."

But as a Christian, you aren't your average person. You are led by the Spirit. So rather than let the thought in, you take it captive. You handcuff it and march it down the street to the courthouse where you present the thought before the judgment seat of Christ.

"Jesus, this thought says I'm a bum and a loser, and that I'll never amount to anything. What do you think?"

See what you are doing? You are submitting the thought to the authority of Jesus. If Jesus agrees with the thought, then let it in. If not, kick it out.

How do you know if Jesus agrees or disagrees? You open your Bible. What does God think about you? Ephesians 2:10 is a good place to check: "For we are God's workmanship, created in Christ Jesus to do good works, which God prepared in advance for us to do" (NIV).

Obviously, any thought that says you are inferior or insignificant does not pass the test—and does not gain entrance. You have the right to give the bully a firm kick in the pants and watch him run.

Let's take another example. The first thought was a bully; this next thought is a groupie. She comes not to tell you how bad you are but how good you are. She rushes to the doorway and gushes, "You are so good. You are so wonderful. The world is so lucky to have you," and on and on the groupie grovels.

Typically, this is the type of thought you'd welcome. But you don't do things the typical way. You guard your heart. You walk in the Spirit. And you take every thought captive. So once again you submit this thought to the authority of Christ. As you search the Word of God, you learn that pride doesn't please God.

"Don't cherish exaggerated ideas of yourself or your importance" (Romans 12:3 PHILLIPS).

As much as you'd like to welcome this thought of conceit into the greenhouse, you can't. You allow only what Christ allows.

One more example. This time the thought is not one of criticism or flattery but one of temptation. It might be that new CD or sweater or video game you've wanted since just about . . . *forever.* There it is, right out on the counter, and the clerk is busy at the other end of the store. Or maybe it's a chance to take a quick peek at a neighbor's test paper, or a tiny puff on that cigarette you promised your folks you'd never smoke. What do you do?

Well, if you aren't under the authority of Christ, you go for it. But if you have the mind of Christ, you step back and say, "Not so fast. You'll have to get permission from my big brother." Then you take the temptation to Jesus and ask, "Yes or no?" Then the answer will come loud and clear.

Guard the doorway of your heart. Submit your thoughts to the authority of Christ. The more choosy you are about seeds, the more delighted you will be with the crop.

> > > Julie studied the sign-up sheet for the new play with delighted eyes. *So many wonderful possibilities!* Then with a smile she handed her pen to the friend at her side. "Here, Cara. You'd be *perfect* for the lead."

"Me?!" asked an astonished Cara—who knew what a smash Julie had been as Maria in last year's production. "But what about you?"

"Well," said Julie, "what goes on behind the scenes is pretty interesting, too, so I'm signing up for the back-stage crew. Besides, it sounds like fun."

A lot of things sounded like—and were—fun these days for the new, positive Julie. Now that she'd let the light in—and worked really hard at keeping the weeds out—Julie's "garden" was turning out to be a fairly gorgeous work-in-progress.

Of course, she did have to keep a careful eye on things. Inside. Where it *all* begins.

11 | FINDING GOLD IN THE GARBAGE

(A HOPE-FILLED HEART)

*Let your hope keep you
joyful, be patient in your
troubles, and pray at all
times.*
—ROMANS 12:12 TEV

> > > "Just look at this place, Scott. Have you ever seen so much . . . *junk?*" Jordan turned slowly, staring with disbelieving eyes at Miss Nelson's enormous, crammed-to-the-rafters attic.

"Not junk," breathed Scott, breaking into a huge grin. "Think of it as possible *treasure.* Isn't it *great?!*"

Jordan barely heard him. What had they gotten themselves into?! She was certain they had bitten off more than they could chew with this service project!

Miss Nelson was ninety years old, and her huge Victorian house had gotten completely out of hand. It needed all kinds of work she couldn't afford. So volunteers from the church had pitched in to clean and fix it up for her. *But, oh, my . . .*

William Rathje likes garbage. This researcher with a degree from Harvard University is convinced we can learn a lot from the trash dumps of the world. Archaeologists have always examined trash to study a society. William Rathje does the same; he just eliminates the wait.

The Garbage Project, as he calls his organization, travels across the country, digging into landfills and recording our eating habits, dress styles, and economic levels (see *American Way Magazine,* 1 April 1992, 32–35). William Rathje is able to find meaning in our garbage.

His organization learned that the average American produces half a pound of trash per day, and the largest landfill in America, located near New York City, has enough trash to fill the Panama Canal. According to Rathje, trash decomposes more slowly than we thought it did. He found a whole steak from 1973 and readable newspapers from the Truman presidency. Rathje learns a lot by looking at our junk.

Reading about Rathje made me wonder, *What is it like to be a "garbologist"?* When he gives a speech, is it called "trash talk"? Are his staff meetings "rubbish reviews"? Are his business trips called "junkets"? When he daydreams about his work, does his wife tell him to get his mind out of the garbage?

Though I prefer to leave the dirty work to Rathje, his attitude toward trash interests me. What if we learned to do the same? Suppose we changed the way we view the garbage that comes our way. After all, don't you have to deal with your share of rubbish? Those chores you dread. Computer foul-ups. Postponed treats.

And then there are the days that a Dumpster couldn't hold all the garbage we face: sickness, disappointments, betrayals. What do you do when an entire truckload of sorrow is dumped on you?

On Rathje's office wall is a framed headline he found in a paper: "Gold in Garbage." This garbologist finds treasure in trash. Jesus did the same. What everyone else saw as disaster, he saw as opportunity. And because he saw what others didn't, he found what others missed.

Early in his ministry Jesus said this about our vision: "Your eyes are windows into your body. If you open your eyes wide in wonder and belief, your body fills up with light. If you live squinty-eyed in greed and distrust, your body is a dank cellar" [Matthew 6:22–23 MSG].

In other words, how we look at life determines how we live life!

> . . . how we look at life determines how we live life!

> > > Jordan sneezed in the cloud of dust stirred up by Scott's *dive* into the wall-to-wall clutter of Miss Nelson's attic. *Doesn't he know this is*

going to be impossible?! Her next sneeze ended in a laugh. *Of course he doesn't, any more than he knows he's . . . short.*

She was right, and she was wrong. It wasn't that Scott wasn't aware he was more . . . vertically challenged? . . . elevation-deprived? . . . okay, *shorter!* . . . than everyone else in the eighth grade. He just didn't see it as a *problem*.

When his lack of inches did cross Scott's mind, it was usually in terms of one more *advantage* it gave him: "I'd be the last one in any crowd to be struck by lightning or a low-flying asteroid, you know." And he was only *half*-kidding. Silver linings in the darkest clouds and lights at the end of the gloomiest tunnels were Scott's specialty.

Scott Monroe was a "lemonade" kind of guy. You know: No matter how sour the "lemons" life might toss at him, Scott would come back with gallons of sweet lemonade—*and*, more often than not, a lemon meringue pie or two! All it took, he was convinced, was digging in and rummaging around until you found what was there all along—something wonderful! Like in this attic, for instance. Scott was *sure* it must hold all kinds of things that Miss Nelson could turn into cash.

"Wow, look at this!" Scott's voice was muffled by the teetering "wall" of old magazines that hid him from Jordan.

"What?" she asked, picking her way cautiously along the trail Scott had blazed that morning.

"Whole sets of really old *National Geographics*," came his enthusiastic reply. "These are worth something for sure. And look at *that*. . . ."

"What now?" Jordan asked, following Scott's voice through the magazine maze.

"Old trunks and furniture and about a bazillion boxes just crammed with . . . stuff," came his delighted answer.

"Where *are* you, Scott?"

"Over here. Keep coming. Oh, and Jordan, be careful of that old harness hanging from the rafters," he warned, only *slightly* too late.

"Honestly, Scott!" she huffed, untangling herself from the smelly old leather. "What on earth do you expect to find in all this . . . this *mess*?" As if she didn't know.

"Treasure," he answered, right on cue. "Got to be plenty of things here that can make a big difference for Miss Nelson."

Goodness knows she could use it, thought Jordan. Everyone knew Miss Nelson's inheritance was about gone, and it looked as if she might have to sell the wonderful old house that had been in her family for generations. But actual *treasure*?

> "Got to be plenty of things here that can make a big difference for Miss Nelson."

"You know, Scott, we're supposed to be cleaning out this junk, not exploring it!"

"Well, sure," came the cheerful reply, "but how can we know we're not throwing out the good with the bad, if we don't *look* first?"

The Darkest Night in History

On the night before his death, a veritable landfill of woes tumbled in on Jesus. Somewhere between the Gethsemane prayer and the mock trial is what has to be the darkest scene in the history of the human drama. Though the entire event couldn't have lasted more than five minutes, it had enough badness to fill a thousand Dumpsters.

Except for Christ, not one person did one good thing. Search the scene for an ounce of courage or a speck of character, and you won't find it. What you will find is a compost heap of deceit and betrayal. Yet in it all, Jesus saw reason to hope. And in his outlook, we find an example to follow.

"Get up, we must go. Look, here comes the man who has turned against me."

While Jesus was still speaking, Judas, one of the twelve apostles, came up. With him were many people carrying swords and clubs who had been sent from the leading priests and the older Jewish leaders of the people. Judas had planned to give them a signal, saying, "The man I kiss is Jesus. Arrest him." At once

Judas went to Jesus and said, "Greetings, Teacher!" and kissed him.

Jesus answered, "Friend, do what you came to do."

Then the people came and grabbed Jesus and arrested him. When that happened, one of Jesus' followers reached for his sword and pulled it out. He struck the servant of the high priest and cut off his ear.

Jesus said to the man, "Put your sword back in its place. All who use swords will be killed with swords. Surely you know I could ask my Father, and he would give me more than twelve armies of angels. But it must happen this way to bring about what the Scriptures say."

Then Jesus said to the crowd, "You came to get me with swords and clubs as if I were a criminal. Every day I sat in the Temple teaching, and you did not arrest me there. But all these things have happened so that it will come about as the prophets wrote." Then all of Jesus' followers left him and ran away.

—MATTHEW 26:46–56 NCV

The darkest night of Jesus' life was marked by one crisis after another. Later we will see what Jesus saw, but first let's consider what an observer would have witnessed in the Garden of Gethsemane.

First he would have seen *unanswered prayer*. Jesus had just offered an anguished appeal to God: "My Father, if it is possible, do not give me this cup of suffering. But do what you want, not what I want" (Matthew 26:39 NCV).

Never has earth offered such an urgent request. And never has heaven offered more deafening silence. The prayer of Jesus was unanswered. *Jesus and unanswered prayer* in the same phrase? How is that possible? Would God, the one who owns the cattle on a thousand hills, keep something from his own Son? He did that night. And that was just the beginning. Look who showed up next.

Judas arrived with an angry crowd. Not only did Jesus have to face unanswered prayer, he also had to deal with *unfruitful service*. The very people he had come to save had now come to arrest him. He came to the aid of so many. All those sermons. All those miracles. And so now we wait for one person who will declare, "Jesus is an innocent man!" But no one does. The people he came to save have turned against him.

We can almost forgive the crowd. Their contact with Jesus was too brief. Perhaps they didn't know better. But the disciples did. They knew better. They knew *him* better. But do they defend Jesus? Hardly. The most bitter pill Jesus had to swallow was the *unbelievable betrayal* by the disciples.

Judas wasn't the only turn-coat. "All of Jesus' followers left him and ran away" (Matthew 26:56 NCV). These are the same people who earlier had echoed Peter's words: "I will never say that I don't know you! I will even die with you!" (Matthew 26:35 NCV).

All pledged loyalty, and yet *all* ran. From the outside looking in, all we see is betrayal. The disciples have left him. The people have rejected him. And God hasn't heard him. Never has so much trash been dumped on one being. From a human point of view, Jesus' world has collapsed.

Jesus, neck-deep in rubbish. That's how I would have described the scene. That's how a witness would have portrayed it. But that's not how Jesus saw it. He saw something else entirely. It wasn't that he didn't see the trash; he just wasn't limited to it. Somehow he was able to see the good in the bad, the purpose in the pain, and God's presence in the problem.

We could use a little of Jesus' 20/20 vision, couldn't we? You and I live in a trashy world. Unwanted garbage comes our way on a regular basis. We, too, have unanswered prayers and unfruitful dreams and unbelievable betrayals, don't we? Haven't you been handed a trash sack of mishaps and heartaches? Sure you have. May I ask, what are you going to do with it?

> > > It took Scott and Jordan—and a dozen dust-covered friends—a month of weekends to clear out the attic. Funny old clothes, tattered books and photos, banged-up furniture, "mystery items" they had no name for. If three generations of Nelsons could save it, there it was. And, armload by armload, box by box, out it all went. But *not* before *first* passing Scott's eagle-eyed inspection.

"What *are* you looking for, Scott?" someone would generally ask.

"Not sure," was always the answer, "but I'll know it when I see it. It's there, guys. All we have to do is keep looking." And Scott would lead the way back into the clutter, and everyone else would shrug and grin and . . . follow.

It was hard work. It was hot work. It was dirty work. What *nobody* could explain was why it was also so *satisfying!* Except maybe Scott—who knew it wasn't *what* you were faced with, but *how* you dealt with it, that mattered. Don't forget, this is the guy measuring five-foot-nothing—and that was on a "tall" day—who had somehow made himself a star basketball player.

Basketball?! Go figure. It might have been an unlikely choice, but Scott was brilliant at it—*and* at turning his close-to-the-ground stature into his biggest asset. "Hey, when you're below their line of sight, the big guys never see you coming!"

What Scott lacked in *altitude*, he more than made up for in attitude—an attitude that leapfrogged from Scott to anyone near him.

Hang out with Scott long enough and you couldn't help but feel strong and confident and . . . hopeful. Which might explain why so many kids looked *up* to the guy whose head barely reached their shoulders.

Seeing What Jesus Sees

You have several options for dealing with the "trash" in *your* life. You could hide it—take the trash bag and cram it under your coat and pretend it isn't there. But you and I know you won't fool anyone. Besides, sooner or later it will start to stink. Or you could disguise it. Paint it green, put it on the front lawn, and tell everybody it is a tree. Again, no one will be fooled.

So what will you do? If you follow the example of Christ, you will learn to see tough times differently. Remember, God loves you just the way you are, but he refuses to leave you that way. He wants you to have a hope-filled heart . . . just like Jesus.

Here is what Christ did.

He found good in the bad. It would be hard to find someone worse than Judas. The Bible says, "Judas . . . was a thief. He was the one who kept the money box, and he often stole from it" (John 12:6 NCV). The man was a crook. Somehow he was able to live in the presence of God and experience the miracles of Christ and remain unchanged. In the end, he sold Jesus for thirty pieces of silver. Judas was a scoundrel, a cheat, and a bum. How could anyone see him any other way?

Jesus did. He looked into the face of his betrayer and said, "Friend, do what you came to do" (Matthew 26:50 NCV). What Jesus saw in Judas as worthy of being called a friend, I can't imagine. But I do know that Jesus doesn't lie, and in that moment he saw something good in a very bad man.

> He wants you to have a hope-filled heart . . . just like Jesus.

It would help if we did the same. But *how?* Again Jesus gives us guidance. He didn't place all the blame on Judas. He saw another presence that night: "This is . . . the time when darkness rules" (Luke 22:53 NCV). In no way was Judas innocent, but neither was Judas acting alone. Your attackers aren't acting alone, either. The powers of darkness are helping things along.

Those who betray us are victims of a fallen world. We needn't place all the blame on them. Jesus found enough good in the face of Judas to call him friend, and he can help us do the same with those who hurt us.

Not only did Jesus find good in the bad, *he found purpose in the pain.* Of the ninety-eight words Jesus spoke at his arrest, thirty refer to the purpose of God.

"It must happen this way to bring about what the Scriptures say" (Matthew 26:54 NCV).

Jesus chose to see his immediate struggle as a necessary part of a greater plan.

I witnessed something similar on a recent flight to St. Louis. Because of storms, our plane was first delayed, then sent to another city where we sat on the runway waiting for the rain clouds to pass. As I was glancing at my watch and drumming my fingers, the fellow across the aisle tapped me on the arm and asked if he could borrow my Bible. I handed it to him. He turned to a young girl sitting next to him, opened the Bible, and the two read the Scriptures for the remainder of the trip.

After some time, the sky cleared, and we resumed our journey. We were landing in St. Louis when he returned the

Bible to me and explained in a low voice that this was the girl's first flight. She'd recently joined the military and was leaving home for the first time. He asked her if she believed in Christ, and she said she wanted to but didn't know how. That's when he borrowed my Bible and told her about Jesus. By the time we landed, she told him she believed in Jesus as the Son of God.

I've since wondered about that event. Did God bring the storm so the girl could hear the gospel? Did God delay our arrival so she'd have plenty of time to learn about Jesus? I wouldn't put it past him. That is how Jesus chose to view the storm that came his way: necessary turbulence in the plan of God. Where others saw gray skies, Jesus saw a divine order.

> > > Even as the last boxes were being carried from the freshly swept—and very empty—attic, Scott still hadn't given up on that elusive *special* "treasure" for Miss Nelson. Oh sure, they'd found a few nice antiques and some rare old books, but—long after everyone else had lost hope—Scott was positive there was still a "big find" waiting to be discovered.

"I must be *missing* something," he assured Jordan with absolute confidence—crossing his arms and leaning against the worn boards of the chimney enclosure. "What we need here is a little imagination . . . some kind of breakthrough—" he began . . . just before he fell through the wall!

"Scott! Are you all right?" Jordan's eyes were enormous as she peered through the broken boards into a tiny hidden room . . . and at a grinning Scott.

"Told you so!" crowed Scott, trying to hold his left arm and lift the lid of a battered old trunk at the same time. "Climb in, Jordan, and give me a hand."

"What's wrong with your arm?"

"Huh? Oh, nothing, just a little numb. Here, help me lift this lid."

Layer by layer, they emptied the trunk. *More old clothes and books and tacky souvenirs—nothing we haven't seen a hundred times already!* thought Jordan, truly sorry to think Scott was going to be disappointed after all.

But for a disappointed guy, Scott was looking remarkably cheerful. In fact, he was positively beaming at some ratty-looking old certificates in the very bottom of the trunk. He couldn't have explained how or why, but he absolutely *knew* . . . this was it!

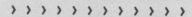

"Well, my goodness," said Miss Nelson, smiling at the group gathered in her freshly painted parlor later that day, "*there* they are."

There what are?!

"I was never sure the story was true," Miss Nelson went on, adding to their confusion.

What story?!

"Well," she explained, "it's always been a family tradition that my great-grandpapa invested in Mr. Edison's 'newfangled' electric company. But we never could find any papers."

"Well," said Jordan's banker father, holding the antique stock certificates *very* carefully, "you've found them now. And they look good as gold. Miss Nelson, your worries are over—you own a piece of a whole *lot* of electric companies!"

"Amazing," said someone. "Incredible," said someone else.

"Told you so," said Scott, nudging Jordan with the cast on his arm.

"But how did you *know?*" she whispered back.

Scott laughed, then said, "Oh, I figured there had to be at least *one* lucky break somewhere in all that mess."

Wouldn't you love to have a hope-filled heart? Wouldn't you love to see the world through the eyes of Jesus? Where we see unanswered prayer, Jesus saw answered prayer. Where we see the absence of God, Jesus saw the plan of God. Remember what he said in Matthew 26:53: "Surely you know I could ask my Father, and he would give me more than twelve armies of angels." Of all the treasures Jesus saw in the trash, this is the most significant. He saw his Father. He saw his Father's presence in the problem. Twelve armies of angels were within his sight.

Sure, Max, but Jesus was God. He could see the unseen. He had eyes for heaven and a vision for the supernatural. I can't see the way he saw.

Not yet maybe, but don't underestimate God's power. He can change the way you look at life.

God never promises to remove us from our struggles. He does promise, however, to change the way we look at them.

God can correct your vision.

He asks, "Who gives a person sight?" then answers, "It is I, the LORD" (Exodus 4:11 NCV). More than one have made the request of the blind man, "Teacher, I want to see" (Mark 10:51 NCV). And more than one have walked away with clear vision. Who is to say that God won't do the same for you?

God can correct your vision.

12 | WHEN HEAVEN CELEBRATES

(A REJOICING HEART)

Sing to the LORD a new song:
*   sing to the LORD, all the earth.*
Sing to the LORD and praise his name;
*   every day tell how he saves us.*
    —PSALM 96:1–2 NCV

Rejoice that your names
are written in heaven.
    —LUKE 10:20 NIV

› › › Her name was Joy, and she was born laughing. Really . . . everyone who was there will swear to it.

When other babies come into the world kicking and screaming, Joy-who-was-*supposed*-to-be-Anabel greeted life with a smile—and what sounded remarkably like a tiny gurgle of delight.

And in all the years that followed, no matter what happened—no matter *what!*—her joyful spirit never changed. Though she never said so, she acted as if she knew some wonderful secret that put a shine on every moment. Her smiles were irresistible . . . her laughter contagious . . . and her friends, many.

And she was driving her foster sister absolutely . . . *NUTS!*

My family did something thoughtful for me last night. They had a party in my honor—a surprise birthday party. Early last week I told my wife not to plan anything except a nice family evening at a restaurant. She listened only to the restaurant part. I had no idea that half a dozen families were going to join us.

In fact, I tried to talk her into staying at home. My daughter Andrea had been sick. Jenna had homework and I'd spent the afternoon watching football games and felt lazy. Not really in a mood to get up and clean up and go out, I thought I'd have no problem convincing "the girls" to postpone the dinner. Boy, was I surprised! They wouldn't think of it. My family made it clear—we were going out to eat.

Not only that, we were leaving on time. I agreed and set about getting ready. But, unfortunately, I moved too slowly! My attitude was, *why hurry?* My daughters' attitude was, *hurry up!* I was ho-hum. They were gung-ho. I was content to stay. They were eager to leave. To be honest, I was bewildered by their actions. They were being surprisingly prompt. Curiously excited. Why the big deal? I mean, I enjoy a night out as much as the next guy, but Sara giggled all the way to the restaurant.

Only when we arrived did their actions make sense. One step inside the door and I understood their enthusiasm. SURPRISE! They knew what I didn't. They had seen what I hadn't. They'd already seen the table and stacked the gifts and smelled the cake. Since they knew about the party, they did everything necessary to see that I didn't miss it.

Jesus does the same for us. He knows about THE PARTY. In one of the greatest chapters in the Bible, Luke 15, he tells three stories. Each story tells of something lost and something found. A lost sheep. A lost coin. And a lost son. And at the end of each one, Jesus describes a party, a celebration. The shepherd throws the party for the lost-now-found sheep. The housewife throws a party because of the lost-now-found coin. And the father throws a party in honor of his lost-now-found son.

Three parables, each with a party. Three stories, each using the same word: *happy*. About the shepherd who found the lost sheep, Jesus says: "And when he finds it, he *happily* puts it on his shoulders and goes home" (vv. 5–6 NCV, italics mine). When the housewife finds her lost coin, she announces, "Be *happy* with me because I have found the coin that I lost" (v. 9 NCV, italics mine). And the father of the prodigal son explains to the reluctant older brother, "We had to celebrate and be *happy* because your brother was dead, but now he is alive. He was lost, but now he is found" (v. 32 NCV, italics mine).

The point is clear. Jesus is happiest when the lost are found. For him, no moment compares to the moment of salvation. For my daughter, the rejoicing began when I got dressed and was in the car and on the road to the party.

Jesus is happiest when the lost are found.

The same occurs in heaven. Let one child consent to be dressed in righteousness and begin the journey home, and heaven pours the punch, strings the streamers, and throws the confetti. "There is joy in the presence of the angels of God when one sinner changes his heart and life" (v. 10 NCV).

> › › › Anyone who knew Joy would have *celebrated* the chance to have her for a foster sister. Anyone, that is, but Liz Carlson. A "veteran" of foster homes—some okay, some *not*-so-okay—Liz saw no reason to get excited about this new one. And even the warm-hearted welcome from Joy and her parents didn't dent her defenses.

At thirteen, Liz already had decided on the Rules of Life: Don't expect anything. Don't count on anyone. Nothing good ever lasts. Keep your guard up.

As philosophies go, it wasn't a very cheery one. But then, Liz had never experienced much to be cheerful *about.* And when it came to treating life like some big *party* (as *some* people did)? *Give me a break!*

It was that life-is-wonderful thing, in fact, that Liz found most annoying about Joy. *Well, sure, it's easy for "Miss Sunshine" to be all happy and cheerful, nothing bad ever happens to* her!

So Liz was polite, Liz was "nice," Liz never let her guard down—no matter how tempting it was to be part of a *real* family. *Besides, they'll soon find some reason to get rid of me anyway, like always.*

She couldn't have been more wrong. Joy's parents actually *liked* the tall, quiet girl with the watchful eyes and the stubborn chin. And Joy—who *always* expected wonderful things to happen—had no intention of letting Liz out of her clutches!

God doesn't make mistakes. He sent Liz to us for a reason! It might have been "Lost Sheep Syndrome" at work, or maybe she saw the Liz-who-*could*-be . . . whatever the reason, Joy's mind was made up. *Life is a gift, and I'm going to get her to celebrate it if it's the last thing I do!*

God doesn't make mistakes. He sent Liz to us for a reason!

How do we explain such heavenly joy over the decision of *one* soul? Why such a stir? You've got to admit the excitement is a bit curious. We aren't talking about a nation of people or even a city of souls; we're talking about joy "when *one* sinner changes his heart and life." How could one person create that much excitement?

Who could imagine that our actions have such an impact on heaven? Our greatest actions on earth go largely unnoticed and unrecorded. Dare we think that God is paying attention?

According to Scripture, he is. According to Jesus, our decisions make a powerful impression on the unseen world. Our actions on the keyboard of earth move hammers on the piano strings of heaven. Our obedience pulls the ropes that ring the bells in heaven's belfries. Let a child call and the ear of the Father hears. Let a sister weep and tears begin to flow from above. And, most important, let a sinner repent, and every other activity stops, and every heavenly being celebrates.

This response to our conversion is remarkable. Heaven throws no party over our other achievements. When we graduate from school or score a winning goal or win an award, as far as we know, the celestial party food stays in the refrigerator. Why the big deal over conversion?

We, on the other hand, don't usually get all that excited about it, do we? When you hear of a soul saved, do you drop everything and celebrate? We might be pleased—but "carried away"? Do we feel an urge to call out the band and cut the cake and have a party? When a soul is saved, the heart of Jesus becomes the night sky on the Fourth of July, filled with explosions of joy.

Can the same be said about us? Perhaps this is one area where our hearts could use some attention.

God's Magnum Opus

Why do Jesus and his angels rejoice over one repenting sinner? Can they see something we can't? Do they know something we don't? Absolutely. They know what heaven holds. They've seen the table, and they've heard the music, and they can't wait to see your face when you arrive. Better still, they can't wait to see you.

When you arrive and enter the party, something wonderful will happen. A final transformation will occur. You will be just like Jesus. "We have not yet been shown what we will be in the future. But we know that when Christ comes again, *we will be like him*" (1 John 3:2 NCV, italics mine).

Of all the blessings of heaven, one of the greatest will be you! You will be God's magnum opus . . . his work of art. The angels will gasp. God's work will be completed. At last, you will have a heart like his.

You will love with a perfect love.

You will worship with a radiant face.

You will hear each word God speaks.

Your heart will be pure, your words will be like jewels, your thoughts will be like treasures.

You will be just like Jesus. You will, at long last, have a heart like his. Picture the heart of Jesus and you'll be picturing your own heart. Guiltless. Fearless. Thrilled and joyous. Tirelessly worshiping. Perfectly understanding. As the mountain stream is pure and endless, so will be your heart. *You will be like him.*

And if that were not enough, everyone else will be like him as well. Heaven is populated by those who let God change them. No wonder the angels rejoice when one sinner repents; they know another work of art will soon grace the gallery of God. They know what heaven holds.

> > > Convincing Liz that God had a plan for her life—that *she* was a masterpiece-in-the-making—was *not* easy. Liz was a *very* tough nut to crack, as her foster family discovered. In fact, anyone but Joy might have said, "Impossible."

Joy, naturally, had an entirely different take on things. *Gonna make me work for this, aren't you, Father? Okay, I know you've got your reasons."* So Joy got busy . . . starting with the "smiling thing."

"Really, Liz, your face won't crack . . . your lips won't go numb . . . the sky won't fall!"

"Don't see much to smile about," Liz would say. Which wasn't entirely true. The longer she was around the warm, loving, *funny* Hamilton family, the harder it was to keep a straight face.

Joy's friends were . . . *nice,* too. Liz hadn't expected that—or the way she was included in everything, like it or not. (She mostly liked it.) The church routine, though? Well, *there* Liz drew the line. What had God ever done for her? (Except, maybe, land her with Joy and her family?)

One thing Liz never got used to was the surprise

celebrations. It seemed the Hamiltons would celebrate *anything!* And always without warning.

"I guess I just don't like surprises," said Liz, who liked to know what was headed her way—just in case it might be necessary to duck.

"Not like surprises?!" Joy was shocked. "But Liz, that's the best part of life—the wonderful *surprises* God sends our way! Like . . . like . . ." Stuck for an example, Joy ran a hand through her shining cap of golden curls. *Aha!* "Like my hair!"

"Your hair?"

"Right. It used to be straight as a stick and all . . . limp," explained Joy with a laugh. "And you should have seen me when I was bald! But afterward, it grew back like *this.*"

"Whoa!" Liz help up a hand. "Bald?!"

"Oh, that was the chemo. The point is, you see, th—"

"Chemo?" Liz thought she might have misunderstood. "But chemo is for . . ."

"Leukemia," said Joy casually—then she took a good look at Liz's shocked face. "Oh, my, of *course* you don't know. Really, it's no big deal. I've been in remission for two years, and it might be gone for good."

"But . . . but you could . . ." Liz couldn't bring herself to say it.

Joy said it for her. "Die?" Liz nodded. Then her mouth dropped open as Joy started to laugh.

"Got a news flash for you, Liz, everybody dies—

sooner or later. That's why it's so important to celebrate every gift God gives us to enjoy while we're here."

"Before . . . before it's . . . over?" asked Liz.

"Goodness, no," said Joy, who was absolutely, positively *sure* of what was waiting on the other side of death. "Before we move on to something incredibly better!" Then she confused Liz even more with her next words. "If, of course, that's what we *choose*. God lets us decide, you know."

"God lets us decide, you know."

There is yet another reason for the celebration when one chooses God. Part of the excitement is from our arrival. The other part is from our deliverance. Jesus rejoices that we are headed to heaven, but he equally rejoices that we are saved from hell.

What We're Saved From

One phrase summarizes the horror of hell: "God isn't there."

Think for a moment about this question: What if God weren't here on earth? You think people can be unkind now, imagine us without the presence of God. You think we are cruel to each other now, imagine the world without the Holy Spirit. You think there is loneliness and despair and guilt now, imagine life without the touch of Jesus. No forgiveness. No hope. No acts of kindness. No words of love. No more food given in his name. No more songs sung to his praise. No more deeds done in his honor. If God took away his angels, his grace, his promise of eternity, and his servants, what would the world be like?

In a word, hell. No one to comfort you and no music to soothe you. A world where poets don't write of love and minstrels don't sing of hope, for love and hope were passengers on the last bus out of town.

According to Jesus, hell knows only one sound, the "weeping and gnashing of teeth" (Matthew 22:13 NIV). From hell comes a woeful, unending moan as its inhabitants realize the opportunity they have missed—the chance to be with God, a chance that is gone forever.

Saved or Lost?

Can you see now why the angels rejoice when one sinner repents? Jesus knows what awaits the saved. He also knows what awaits the condemned. Can you see why we should rejoice, too? How can we? How can our hearts be changed so we rejoice as Jesus rejoices?

Ask God to help you have his eternal view of the world. His view of humanity is very simple. His list is very basic. From God's perspective, every person is either saved . . . or lost.

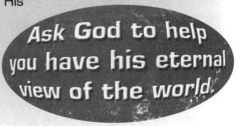

Ask God to help you have his eternal view of the world.

People, on the other hand, keep much more *complicated* lists on each other. Is he rich? Is she pretty? What kind of grades does he get? What color is her skin? Is she talented? Is he popular? God doesn't care about things like these. And as he shapes us more and more to be like Jesus, they become less and less important to us as well.

To have a heart like his is to look into the faces of the saved and rejoice! They are just one grave away from being just like Jesus. To have a heart like his is to look into the faces of the lost and pray. For unless they turn, they are one grave away from torment.

And so my challenge to you is simple. Ask God to help you have his *eternal* view of the world. To see as he sees. To know what is really important.

Every person you meet has been given an invitation to the party. When one says yes, celebrate! And when one acts sluggish as I did, do what my daughters did. Stir him up and urge him to get ready. It's almost time for the party . . . it would be a shame for anyone to miss it!

〉 〉 〉 It took Liz a while to wrap her mind—and heart—around the things Joy had told her, especially that last part:

"None of us get to decide how long we'll be here, Liz. But we *do* get to choose what we'll do with our lives . . . how we'll *celebrate* the gift . . . and where we'll be going next."

Choose? I get to choose?!

Other people had always decided things for Liz, so the idea that the really *important* choices were always hers was a little . . . strange. But, come to think of it, no stranger than a girl with leukemia who jumped into every day as if it were some fabulous *gift* hand-delivered by God!

Choose? I *get* to choose?!

Liz couldn't help but smile (Yes!) these days when she thought about Joy—and the way she insisted on *sharing* the gift with anyone who wandered by. Especially Liz.

So, what if she's right? Liz started wondering. *What if there is a gift . . . and what if there's one for me, too?*

Almost without noticing, Liz stopped dwelling on old pains . . . and started looking for new joys. She also started looking for *God* in the things that happened. She even started talking *to* God. A little. Now and then. And that felt so good that she found herself turning to God more and more often. Finally, she chose to turn her life over to God completely. And with his help, she gradually said good-bye to the old Liz and started working on the new-and-improved Liz.

She even enjoyed the surprise party Joy threw for her—after the initial shock, that is.

"It's your *un*-birthday party, Liz. Just because . . . well, you know . . ."

"I know, Miss Sunshine . . . just because it's time to celebrate *something.*" Which was fine with Liz, who was starting to get into this whole "celebration" thing.

13 | GOING THE DISTANCE

(AN ENDURING HEART)

*Let us run the race
that is before us
and never give up.*
　　　　—HEBREWS 12:1 NCV

›　›　› The graffiti-bold, in-your-face notice on the door practically *dared* you to ignore it. "**Team Sign-ups. ONLY THE STRONG NEED APPLY!**" it challenged.

Jameel, Carlos, and Anton traded looks and grins. "Gotta mean *us!*" they agreed—though they had no idea *what* team. Didn't matter, they were up for *anything!* (You *had* to be strong to make it in *their* neighborhood!)

So, laughing and shoving and flexing invisible "muscles," they strutted into New Hope Community Center to sign up for . . . whatever. *Hey, if we don't like it, we can always quit!* (Or so they thought—until they met Miguel Rodriguez, who had his own take on the subject of quitting when the going got tough.)

On one of my shelves is a book on power abs. The cover shows a closeup of a fellow flexing his flat belly. His stomach has more ripples and ridges than a pond on a windy day. Inspired, I bought the book, read the routine, and did the sit-ups . . . for a week.

Not far from the power-abs book is a tape series on speed-reading. It promises to do for my mind what *Power Abs* promised to do for my belly—turn it into steel. All I have to do is listen to the tapes—and I will . . . someday.

And then there is my bottle of essential minerals. Thirty-two ounces of pure health. (There's even a trace of iron, which is good since I missed my shot at the iron abs and the steel-trap mind.) I just keep forgetting to take them.

Any unfinished projects on your list?

Don't get me wrong. Not everything in my life is incomplete. But I confess, I don't always finish what I start. Chances are, I'm not alone.

Any unfinished projects on your list? Perhaps an unopened learn-to-play-guitar-in-just-eight-weeks video or unread success-in-soccer book? How about a half-complete history project or half-mown lawn? And let's not even touch the topic of diets and exercise, okay?

You know as well as I, it's one thing to start something; it's something else entirely to complete it. You might think I'm going to talk to you about the importance of finishing everything. Could be you are bracing yourself for a bit of scolding.

If so, relax. "Don't start what you can't finish" is not one of my points. To be honest, I don't believe you *should* finish everything you start. (Every student with homework just perked up.) There are certain quests better left undone, some projects wisely abandoned. (Though I wouldn't list homework as one of those.)

We can become so focused on finishing that we overlook the question of importance. Just because a project is on the table doesn't mean it can't be returned to the shelf. No, my desire is not to convince you to finish everything. My desire is to encourage you to finish the *right* thing. Certain races are optional—like washboard abs and speed-reading. Other races are essential—like the race of faith. Consider this advice from the author of Hebrews: "Let us run the race that is before us and never give up" (Hebrews 12:1 NCV).

> ❯ ❯ ❯ "You want us to do *WHAT?!*" an indignant Jameel asked the compact, wiry man at the sign-up table.
>
> "Yeah," chimed in Anton, "we thought this would be football or maybe boxing. How's a sissy game like soccer gonna help us get out of the 'hood?"
>
> Carlos was amazingly quiet—but then, he knew a

lot more than his two friends did about what kind of game soccer *really* was.

Coach Rodriguez just smiled and shrugged. "Oh, well . . . if you're not *up* to the game."

Not up to it? Not up to some prance-around-the-field game they play in the suburbs?! Ha! Just like that, Miguel Rodriguez had his first three soccer players for the team he had long dreamed of forming. The energetic businessman, and part-time youth coach, had grown up in a neighborhood very much like the boys'. He knew the temptations they faced every day—the way gangs and drugs offered a "quick fix" for feelings of anger and hopelessness. Team sports had turned *his* life around, and he wanted to share the gift—*and* the life-lessons he'd learned about "choosing your battles" and finishing the *right* things.

Once he'd hooked Jameel, Carlos, and Anton on the idea, their friends soon followed. And it wasn't long before the Riverdale Youth Soccer League had its first inner-city team: the Amigos. In the months that followed, it all turned out to be an enlightening experience for everyone involved.

Coach Rodriguez got to teach a lot more than soccer fundamentals—which was the idea all along. The members of the Elm Hill Church team—who had volunteered to help the Amigos—got to know some kids whose lives were not at all like theirs. And Jameel and his friends discovered that being "strong" and "tough" takes a lot more than just muscle.

The Race

The Christian's race is not a jog in the park but rather a demanding and difficult, sometimes agonizing, race. It takes a massive effort to finish strong.

Likely you've noticed that many people don't. Surely you've observed there are many on the side of the trail. They used to be running. There was a time when they kept the pace. But then weariness set in. They didn't think the run would be this tough. Or they were discouraged by a bump or psyched out by a fellow runner.

Whatever the reason, they don't run anymore. They might be Christians. They might come to church, but their hearts aren't in the race. They retired before their time. Unless something changes, their best work will have been their first work, and they will finish with a whimper.

By contrast, Jesus' best work was his final work, and his strongest step was his last step. Our Master is the classic example of one who endured. The writer of Hebrews goes on to say that Jesus "held on while wicked people were doing evil things to him" (v. 3). The Bible says Jesus "held on," implying that he could have "let go." The runner could have given up, sat down, gone home. He could have quit the race. But he didn't.

> ❯ ❯ ❯ Trapping. Heading. Marking. Dribbling. "Man . . . why does everything have to have a *name?* What difference does that stuff make, long as we get the ball in the goal?!" That was Jameel, who liked to get on with things.

"Well," Coach Rodriguez said patiently, "it's knowing that stuff—and *doing* it—that makes it possible to *get* the ball in the goal."

"No, Carlos! Not like that . . . like this." And Annie Reynolds' flying feet would whisk the ball out from under him and dance it down the field. *A girl? I'm getting help from a twelve-year-old girl?!*

"Tell you what, Carlos," Annie said, reading his face, "when you can steal the ball *back* from this twelve-year-old girl, we'll call it quits." And she'd steal it *again* from him!

"What do you mean, I can't use my hands?!"

"Sorry, Anton, hands not allowed. But . . . ," Mike Carter said with a grin, "you can use everything *else*." And he demonstrated a perfect chest trap and worked with Anton till *he* got it.

> "What do you mean, I can't use my hands?!"

> > > > > > > > > > > >

Those first weeks of soccer fundamentals were a real eye-opener for the Amigos. First of all, there was a lot more to soccer than "prancing around the field." There were skills to master. ("You can hit the ball with your head?") And strategy to understand. ("Where'd he come from?") And rules . . . lots of rules—and Coach Rodriguez was a stickler for every single one. He was also big on sticking to whatever they were struggling with until they got it. No giving up allowed!

"How are we ever going to win with all these rules and other stuff getting in the way?" asked a frustrated Anton.

"Is that what you think this is about?" Coach Rodriguez asked. "Just winning?"

Huh?! "What else could it be about?" asked a puzzled Jameel. In *his* neighborhood, coming out on top was *all* that mattered.

"Thought you'd never ask," said Coach, with a smile. "You want a way out of the 'hood, right?" They nodded. "Well, there it is," he said, pointing at the soccer field. They still didn't get it.

"Scores aren't *all* that count," he told them. "They're an 'outside' thing. What this game or school—or *life*—is about is what's *inside* you. How hard you're willing to work. How long you'll stick it out. How determined you are to hang in till the very end—no matter how tough things get." Then he grinned. "Of course, if you're not *up* to it . . ."

Quit? Us? No way!

That did it . . . again. *Quit? Us? No way!* Of course, that was easier *said* than *done.*

More than once the three boys came very close to throwing up their hands and walking away from this frustrating sport—with quick-tempered Jameel (who didn't like losing) leading the way! But when push came to shove—and it sometimes did—Anton and

Carlos made it clear they wanted to see this "soccer thing" through to the end.

"Don't you guys know when to give up?" Jameel grumbled. Then, with a sigh, he added, "Okay, we always stuck together. No point changing that now."

The Resistance

Can you think of times when Jesus could have given up? How about his time of temptation? You and I know what it is like to endure a moment of temptation or an hour of temptation, even a day of temptation. But *forty* days? That is what Jesus faced. "The Spirit led Jesus into the desert where the devil tempted Jesus for forty days" (Luke 4:1–2 NCV).

Jesus' time of testing was nonstop. Satan got on Jesus like a shirt and refused to leave. Every step, whispering in his ear. Every turn of the path, sowing doubt.

Was Jesus affected by the devil? Apparently so. Luke doesn't say Satan *tried* to tempt Jesus. No, the passage is clear: "the devil *tempted* Jesus." Jesus was *tempted;* he was *tested.* Tempted to change sides? Tempted to go home? Tempted to settle for a kingdom on earth? I don't know, but I know he was tempted. A war raged within. Stress stormed without. And since he was tempted, he could have quit the race. But he didn't. He kept on running.

Temptation didn't stop him, nor did accusations. Can you imagine what it would be like to run in a race and be criticized by the bystanders?

Some years ago I entered a five-K race. Nothing serious,

just a jog through the neighborhood to raise funds for a charity. Not being the wisest of runners, I started off at an impossible pace. Within a mile I was sucking air. At the right time, however, the spectators encouraged me. Sympathetic onlookers urged me on. I had never seen these people, but that didn't matter. I needed a voice of encouragement, and they gave it. And I kept going.

What if in the toughest steps of the race, I had heard words of accusation and not encouragement? And what if the accusations came not from strangers I could dismiss but from my neighbors and family?

That's what happened to Jesus. His own family called him a lunatic. His neighbors treated him even worse. But Jesus didn't quit running. Temptations didn't deter him. Accusations didn't defeat him. Nor did shame dishearten him.

I invite you to think carefully about the supreme test Jesus faced in the race. Hebrews 12:2 offers this interesting statement: "[Jesus] accepted the shame as if it were nothing" (NCV).

Shame is a feeling of disgrace, embarrassment, humiliation. Forgive me for stirring the memory, but don't you have a shameful moment in your history? What if a videotape of that event were played before your family and friends? How would you feel?

That is exactly what Jesus felt. *Why?* you ask. *He never did anything worthy of shame.* No, but *we* did! And since on the cross God made him become sin (2 Corinthians 5:21), Jesus was covered with shame. He was shamed before his family. Shamed before his fellowmen. Shamed before his church. Shamed before the city of Jerusalem. Condemned to die a criminal's death.

But the shame before men didn't compare with the shame Jesus felt before his Father. Our individual shame seems too much to bear. Can you imagine bearing the combined shame of all humanity? One wave of shame after another was dumped on Jesus. Though he never cheated, he was convicted as a cheat. Though he never stole, heaven regarded him as a thief. Though he never lied, he was considered a liar. Though he never lusted, he bore the shame of an adulterer. Though he always believed, he endured the disgrace of an infidel.

Such words stir one urgent question: How? How did he endure such disgrace? What gave Jesus the strength to endure the shame of all the world? We need an answer, don't we? Like Jesus, we are tempted. Like Jesus, we are accused. Like Jesus, we are ashamed. But unlike Jesus, we give up. We give out. We sit down. How can we keep running as Jesus did? How can our hearts have the endurance Jesus had?

By focusing where Jesus focused: on "the joy that God put before him" (Hebrews 12:2 NCV).

> > > "Look ahead, Amigos . . . always look *ahead!*" Coach Rodriguez had said it so often his team members heard it in their sleep. And it wasn't just soccer he was talking about—they'd pretty much caught on to that.

Of course, being both human *and* a coach, Miguel Rodriguez wouldn't have minded if they made progress *on* the soccer field, as well as off it—maybe even scored a goal now and then. Which, so far, had yet to happen.

"Man, we're *terrible!*" That was Anton, trying for the umpteenth time to master the heel pass.

"No problem," said Carlos. "We can get better."

"Only direction we *can* go," agreed Jameel with a grimace—and a grin.

And that was the amazing thing: The Amigos might not have been much of a soccer team now, but they had made up their minds—even Jameel, *especially* Jameel—that they were going to be. Whatever it took! And it took quite a lot. But with the help and encouragement of their coach and the other teams they were making progress. No, they weren't "good" yet, but they were getting *better* all the time. And that *was* something. A big something.

Kids who'd always looked out for "number one" were discovering teamwork. Kids who'd never stuck to anything were learning what happens when you do— and that was showing at home and school, as well as the soccer field. Kids who'd never seen much future for themselves now understood that their future was theirs to decide—if they stayed the course!

The Amigos, in fact, were the talk of the Youth Soccer League. Kids and parents who had their doubts about having these inner-city kids in their league were now their biggest fans. They applauded the way the Amigos never gave up. They admired the way they made the teams that beat them (every one) work for every victory. And when the Amigos finally scored their first-ever goal, everyone—including the other team—cheered.

And the Amigos? Well, they liked the feeling so much they decided they wanted a lot more of it. Of course, they'd have to work for it.

"No problem . . . ," said Carlos.

"Piece of cake . . . ," added Anton.

"What are we waiting for?" finished Jameel.

The Reward

Jesus focused on "the joy that God put before him" (Hebrews 12:2 NCV). This Scripture verse might very well be the greatest testimony ever written about the glory of heaven. Nothing is said about golden streets or angels' wings. No mention is made of music or feasts. Even the word *heaven* is missing from the verse. But though the word is missing, the power is not.

Remember, heaven was not foreign to Jesus. He is the only person to live on earth *after* he had lived in heaven. As believers, you and I will live in heaven after time on earth, but Jesus did just the opposite. He knew heaven before he came to earth. He knew what awaited him upon his return. And knowing what awaited him in heaven enabled him to bear the shame on earth.

In his final moments, Jesus focused on the joy God put before him. He focused on the prize of heaven. By focusing on the prize, he was able not only to finish the race but to finish it strong.

I'm doing my best to do the same. In a far less important ordeal, I, too, am seeking to finish strong. Writing a book is much like running a long race. There is the initial burst of enthusiasm. Then the sags of energy. You give serious thought to giving up, but then a chapter will surprise you with a downhill slope. Occasionally, an idea will inspire you. Often a chapter will tire you. But most of the work has the rhythm of a long-distance runner: long, sometimes lonely stretches at a steady pace.

And toward the end, with the finish line in sight, there comes a numbing of the senses. You want to finish strong. You reach deep for the intensity you had months earlier, but the supply is scarce. The words blur and the mind numbs. You need a kick, you need a surge, you need inspiration.

You want to finish strong.

May I tell you where I find it? (This might sound peculiar, but bear with me.) Through years of writing, I've developed a ritual. Upon completion of a project, I enjoy a rite of celebration. It involves two phases.

The first is a quiet moment before God. The moment the manuscript is in the mail, I find a secluded spot and stop. I don't say much, and, at least so far, neither does God. The purpose is not to talk as much as it is to relish. To delight in the sweet satisfaction of a completed task. For a few moments, God and I savor it together.

Then (and this might really sound boring), I eat. One year it was a Mexican dinner on the San Antonio River. Another year it was room service and a basketball game. Last year I had catfish at a roadside café. The food might vary, but one rule remains constant. Throughout the meal I allow myself only one thought. *I am finished.* Planning future projects is not permitted. Thoughts of tomorrow's tasks are not allowed. I indulge myself in a make-believe world and pretend that my life's work is complete.

And during that meal, in a tiny way, I understand where Jesus found his strength. He lifted his eyes beyond the horizon and saw the table. He focused on the feast. And what he saw gave him strength to finish—and finish strong.

Such a moment awaits us. We will be seated at God's table, and Christ will christen the meal with these words: "Well done, good and faithful servant" (Matthew 25:23 KJV).

And in that moment, the race will have been worth it.

› › › For the team that finished dead last—but *did* finish—it was a great season. There was, to their astonishment, even a trophy for the Amigos at the year-end banquet!

"**Most Improved Team—ONLY THE STRONG NEED APPLY!**" read the plaque.

14 | FIXING YOUR EYES ON JESUS

(THE HEART OF THE MATTER)

May he enlighten the eyes of
your mind so that you can see
what hope his call holds for you,
what rich glories the saints will
inherit.
—EPHESIANS 1:18 TJB

There are times when we see. And there are times when
we *see*. Let me show you what I mean:

Everything changes the day you see the "50 percent off"
sign on that racing bike you've dreamed of for a year. All
of a sudden nothing else matters. You sigh as you behold
your dream. You run your fingers over the sleek frame,
pausing only to wipe the drool from your shirt. As you
gaze, you are transported, and it's just you and your
dream bike and the wind in your face.

Or perhaps the following paragraph better describes you:

Everything changes the day you see him enter the classroom. The new student has just enough swagger to be cool. Just enough smarts to be classy. Not walking so fast as to be nervous, nor so slow as to be cocky. You've seen him before, but only in your dreams. Now he's really here. And you can't take your eyes off him.

There are times when we see. And then there are times when we *see*. There are times when we observe, and times when we memorize. There are times when we notice, and there are times when we study. Most of us know what it means to see a new bike or a new boy . . . but do we know what it's like to see Jesus? Do we know what it's like to "fix our eyes on Jesus" (Hebrews 12:2 NIV)?

We've spent the previous chapters looking at what it means to be just like Jesus. The world has never known a heart so pure, a character so flawless. His spiritual hearing was so keen he never missed a heavenly whisper. His mercy so abundant he never missed a chance to forgive. No lie left his lips, no distraction marred his vision. He touched when others avoided. He endured when others quit.

Jesus is the ultimate model for every person. And what we have done in these pages is precisely what God invites you to do with the rest of your life. He urges you to fix your eyes on Jesus. Heaven invites you to set the lens of your heart on the heart of the Savior and make him the focus of your life.

> > > *What a mess!* thought Jessie, her eyes fixed on the face frowning back at her from the mirror.

There was a time when Jessie—a very *little* Jessie—loved looking into mirrors. She couldn't get enough of Jessie-making-faces, Jessie-striking-poses, Jessie-being-*Jessie*. But the older she grew, the less satisfied she was with the Jessie *she* saw. Such an . . . *ordinary* . . . face; such an ordinary girl.

By the time Jessie was thirteen, *nothing* about her reflection pleased her. A mop of hair she couldn't do a thing with! (Never mind that it was a curly "mop" that covered a very sharp mind.) Eyes that didn't quite fit her thin, angular face. (Never mind that they were a beautiful gray, with a talent—had she used it more—for seeing the funny side of things.) A skinny, awkward body with absolutely no shape. (Never mind that it held a kind heart and generous spirit.) A zit here, braces there . . . on and on went Jessie's list, till all she saw were flaws.

Yuck! It's amazing I have any *friends!* But she did, quite a few actually—and one in particular who was about to seriously shake up Jessie's thinking.

Jessie was looking at all the wrong things . . .

The thing was, you see, Jessie was looking at all the wrong things . . . looking in entirely the wrong direction . . . and not *seeing* at all.

We've talked about *seeing* Jesus . . . but what does that mean?

The shepherds can tell us. For them it wasn't enough to see the angels. You'd think it would have been. The night sky shattered with light and song. Simple shepherds roused from their sleep and raised to their feet by a choir of angels: "Glory to God in the highest!"

But it wasn't enough to see the angels. The shepherds wanted to see the one who sent the angels. Since they wouldn't be satisfied until they saw him, you can trace the long line of Jesus-seekers to a person of the pasture who said, "Let's go. . . . Let's *see*" (Luke 2:15 NCV, italics mine).

"Glory to God in the highest!"

Not far behind the shepherds was a man named Simeon. Luke tells us Simeon was a good man who served in the Temple, who "had been told by the Holy Spirit that he would not die before he saw the Christ promised by the Lord" (Luke 2:26 NCV).

This prophecy was fulfilled only a few days after the shepherds saw Jesus. Somehow Simeon knew the blanketed bundle he saw in Mary's arms was the Almighty God. And for Simeon, seeing Jesus was enough. Now he was ready to die. Some don't want to die until they've seen the world. Simeon didn't want to die until he had seen the Maker of the world.

The wise men had the same desire. Like Simeon, they wanted to see Jesus. Like the shepherds, they were not satisfied with what they saw in the night sky. It wasn't enough to see the light over Bethlehem; they had to see the Light of Bethlehem.

And they succeeded! They all succeeded. More remarkable than their diligence was Jesus' _willingness._ Jesus wanted to be seen! Search for one example of one person who desired to see the infant Jesus and was turned away. You won't find it.

You will find examples of those who didn't seek him. Those, like King Herod, who were content with less. Those, like the religious leaders, who preferred reading about him to seeing him. The ratio between those who missed him and those who sought him is thousands to one. But the ratio between those who sought him and those who found him was one to one. _All who sought him found him._

Or consider John and Andrew. For them it wasn't enough to listen to John the Baptist. Most would have been content to serve in the shadow of the world's most famous evangelist. Could there be a better teacher? Only one. And when John and Andrew saw him, they left John the Baptist and followed Jesus. Note the request they made.

"Rabbi," they asked, "where are you staying?" (John 1:38 NCV). It was a pretty bold request. They didn't ask Jesus to give them a minute or a message or a miracle. They asked for his address. They wanted to hang out with him. They wanted to know him.

They wanted to see him. They wanted to know what made him laugh and if he ever got tired. Most of all, they wanted to know, _Could Jesus be who John said he was—and if he is, what on earth is God doing on the earth?_ You can't answer such a question by talking to his cousin; you've got to talk to the man himself.

Jesus' answer to the disciples? "Come and see" (v. 39). He didn't say, "Come and glance," or "Come and peek." He said, "Come and see." Bring your bifocals and binoculars. This is no time for side-glances or occasional peeks.

The racer fixes his eyes on the bike. The girl fixes her eyes on the boy. The disciple fixes his eyes on the Savior.

> > > "My goodness, Jessie," said Carly, watching her friend frown at her reflection in the shop window, "you certainly are picky about what God spent so much time on."

What?! Jessie's eyes flew from the window to her smiling friend. "Come on, Carly. I know you're a strong Christian and all, but you know and I know that God did *not* make that tacky sweater!"

"No," said Carly with a grin, "he's probably got better taste than that. But then, it wasn't the sweater you were looking at, was it?"

Caught! "No," sighed Jessie, who had long ago given up on fooling her friend, "it wasn't. I was just . . . you know . . . checking out *me.*" Then it struck her—what Carly had said about God spending time on . . . "Me?! You're saying God spent time on *me?*"

"Me?! You're saying God spent time on me?"

"Of course, he did . . . and does. Why don't you come to church with me and find out more?" Carly asked.

It was just another in a long line of invitations from Carly, who was determined to share the very best part of her life with her very best friend. Fortunately, she was as persistent as Jessie was resistant. It wasn't that Jessie didn't respect her friend's beliefs, it was just that Jessie's family wasn't at all . . . church-y.

"Oh, Jess," said Carly, "I wish you could see yourself the way God sees you!"

"The way *God* sees me?! I don't understand," said Jessie with a thoughtful look at her reflection in the window. "Okay, I'll come once—" she said, to Carly's absolute amazement. "But just once. After all, what have I got to lose?"

"Or, maybe," said Carly, once she caught her breath, "a better question is: What have you got to *find?*"

Of course, to find, you have to *seek.* That's what Matthew did. Matthew, if you remember, was converted at work. According to his résumé, he was a revenue consultant for the government. According to his neighbors, he was a crook. He kept a tax booth and a hand extended at the street corner. That's where he was the day he saw Jesus. "Follow me," the Master said, and Matthew did. And in the very next verse we find Jesus sitting at Matthew's dining room table.

A curbside conversion couldn't satisfy his heart, so

Matthew took Jesus home. It didn't matter to Jesus that Matthew was a thief. What did matter was that Matthew wanted to know Jesus, and he was rewarded with the presence of Christ in his home.

Of course, it only made sense that Jesus spend time with Matthew. After all, Matthew was a top draft pick, shoulder-tapped to write the first book of the New Testament. Jesus hangs out with only the big guys like Matthew and Andrew and John. Right?

Wrong! Zacchaeus was far from a big guy. He was small, so small he couldn't see over the crowd that lined the street the day Jesus came to Jericho. But he, like Matthew, had a hunger in his heart to see Jesus.

It wasn't enough to listen to someone else describe the parade of the Messiah. Zacchaeus wanted to see Jesus with his own eyes.

So he went out on a limb. Clad in a three-piece Armani suit and brand-new Italian loafers, he shinnied up a tree in hopes of seeing Christ.

Would you be willing to go out on a limb to see Jesus?

I wonder, would *you* be willing to go out on a limb to see Jesus? Not everyone would. In the same Bible where we read about Zacchaeus crawling across the limb, we read about a young ruler. Unlike Zacchaeus, the crowd parted to make room for the young ruler. He was the . . . ahem . . . *rich*, young ruler. Upon learning that Jesus was in the area, he called for the limo and cruised across town and approached the Carpenter. Please note the question *he* had for Jesus: "Teacher, what good thing must I do to have life forever?" (Matthew 19:16 NCV).

Bottom-line sort of fellow, this ruler. "Let's get right to the issue. Your schedule is busy; so is mine. Tell me how I can get saved, and I'll leave you alone."

There was nothing wrong with this question, but there was a problem with his heart. Contrast his desire with that of Zacchaeus, "Can I make it up that tree?"

▸▸ Or John and Andrew, "Where are you staying?"

▸▸ Or Matthew, "Can you spend the evening?"

▸▸ Or Simeon, "Can I stay alive until I see him?"

▸▸ Or the wise men, "Saddle up the camels. We aren't stopping until we find him."

▸▸ Or the shepherd, "Let's go. . . . Let's *see*."

See the difference? The rich, young ruler wanted medicine. The others wanted the physician. The ruler wanted an answer to his quiz. They wanted the teacher. He was in a hurry. They had all the time in the world. He settled for a cup of coffee at the drive-through window. They wouldn't settle for anything less than a full-course meal at the banquet table. They wanted more than salvation. They wanted the Savior. They wanted to see Jesus.

> > > "Wait till you see, Jess . . . wait till you *see!*" Carly could barely contain her delight at Jessie's agreement to come to church with her—even if it was only just to . . . see.

> > > > > > > > > > > >

Church was—and wasn't—what Jessie had expected. Yes, there was praying and preaching and singing. But no, it wasn't at all dull or boring or . . . embarrassing. In fact, Jessie had to admit, it was actually kind of . . . uplifting. Everyone was friendly and welcoming, and some of the things she heard got Jessie wondering . . . about a *lot* of things.

So "once" became "just once more."

"Of course," purred Carly. "Whatever you say, Jess."

After many more "once mores," Jessie just stopped counting—and threw her heart into getting to know God and his Son—Jesus. And the more she learned, the more she wanted to know. It was all so . . . amazing. *Carly was right!* Who would have dreamed that God put so much value on each person . . . on *her?* Who could have imagined someone like Jesus, and the sacrifice he made . . . for *her?* And who would ever dare hope to feel so loved, and accepted, and treasured . . . *just as she was?*

The more Jessie learned to look past outside things, the closer she came to seeing herself as God saw her—his beloved child, filled to the brim with gifts and talents and possibilities.

Amazing! Jessie smiled at her reflection in the mirror. *Such a change!* Oh, the hair was still a mess, the braces were still there, she was still all arms and legs. The outside hadn't changed at all, but she didn't worry about those things anymore! On the inside, Jessie knew she was blessed with such riches that she really didn't feel at all ordinary anymore.

The disciples found Jesus because they looked for him. They *saw* him because they searched for him—earnestly, sincerely, *diligently.*

Diligent—what a great word! Be diligent in *your* search. Be hungry in your quest, relentless in your pilgrimage. Let this book be but one of dozens you read about Jesus and this hour be but one of hundreds in which you seek him.

Don't be satisfied with angels. Don't be content with stars in the sky. Seek him out as the shepherds did. Long for him as Simeon did. Worship him as the wise men did. Do as John and Andrew did: Ask for his address. Do as Matthew did: Invite Jesus into your house. Imitate Zacchaeus: Risk whatever it takes to see Christ.

God rewards those who seek *him.* Many settle for lesser passions, but the reward goes to those who settle for nothing less than Jesus himself. And what is the

God rewards those who seek him.

reward? What awaits those who seek Jesus? Nothing short of the heart of Jesus. "And as the Spirit of the Lord works within us, we become more and more like him" (2 Corinthians 3:18 TLB).

Can you think of a greater gift than to be like Jesus? Christ felt no guilt; God wants to banish yours. Jesus had no bad habits; God wants to remove yours. Jesus had no fear of death; God wants you to be fearless. Jesus had kindness for the diseased and mercy for the rebellious and courage for the challenges. God wants you to have the same.

He loves you just the way you are, but he refuses to leave you that way.

He wants you to be . . .

JUST LIKE JESUS

WHAT I AM DOING TO BE JUST LIKE JESUS . . .

In your lives you must think
and act like Christ Jesus.
Christ himself was like
God in everything.
—PHILIPPIANS 2:5–6 (ICB)

HOW I AM BECOMING THE HANDS OF JESUS . . .

Let the teaching of Christ live in you richly. Use all wisdom to teach and strengthen each other.
—COLOSSIANS 3:16 (ICB)

Share the "Just Like Jesus" Message with Every Age

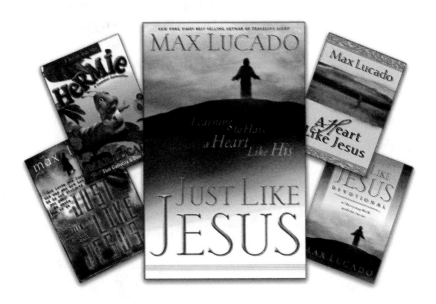

From Max Lucado
America's Leading Inspirational Author

FOR CHILDREN

Hermie: A Common Caterpillar
(VHS / DVD)

Hermie: A Common Caterpillar
(board book)

Hermie: A Common Caterpillar
(picture book)

(Hermie products also available in Spanish)

FOR TWEENS

Just Like Jesus

FOR YOU

Just Like Jesus (hardcover book)
(Also available in Spanish)

Just Like Jesus Devotional

A Heart Like Jesus